To Barb + B...
Enjoy
D. Gail

1

Who Knew?

Milford Writers

Barbara Armstrong, Marnie Dooling, Max Kirschke, Gail Koch, Debbie Shew and Connie Sypniewski

Foreword by Susan McCoy

Cover Design by Gail Koch

Group Picture by Bob Koch

Publishing Consultant: Susan McCoy

Milford Writer's Press

Milford, Michigan

Milford Writers Press

1050 Atlantic Street

Milford, Michigan 48381

Cover design: Gail Koch

ISBN-13:9781537660585

ISBN-10:1537660586

Thank you to Nancy Hinzmann – Director of Milford Senior Center. From the beginning of this writing project, she has offered encouragement and support. We are grateful.

Our cover design by Gail Koch would not have been possible in digital form without the dedicated effort of Bob Koch. Thank you.

Foreword

In the summer, I live on an island with no street lights. Walking the lane at night requires the shimmer of the moon or a flashlight in order to arrive at my destination. Words on a page can be like that providing a ray of connection from one soul to another spanning time and place. There are many celebratory and dark days in life; writing can offer hope, observation, remembrance, and understanding.

For the past three years, I have had the delight of facilitating a weekly Creative Process Workshop held in the Milford Senior Center. Each attendee desired to reflect on life through the art of writing. At first, meetings focused on the mystery of inspiration. In preparation, I researched the thoughts of published authors. During seminar, I shared what examined essayists had to say about listening and recording ideas.

The home assignment was to sit before a blank page and trust that a unique voice would beam within. As insight channeled through, the writer guided their pen or fingers on the keyboard to document without judgment every word until the page was ablaze with words. The next session, writers would read aloud what they had written and listeners would offer their thoughts. By reading-out-loud, the writer could hear what was missing. Changes were made, the re-writes began with one word, two words, and then full sentences until pens or keyboarding were energized beyond what we previously believed possible. The Milford Writers had something to say and they trusted their muse to guide them. We became charmed by the process.

After the first year we took a break to enjoy summer. In the fall, the writer's returned. Notebooks filled. We discovered that often the topic we thought we wanted to write about was not the story that clamored to be heard. That insight was noted and those stories became alive on the page.

Personally, I have experienced joy working with this group. No matter what was happening in life, Tuesday with the Milford Writers delivered possibility laced with an adrenaline rush.

This anthology is an act of trust and should be read as work in progress. Stories are being shared with the hope of illuminating a path for themselves and perhaps a reader or two.

The significance of our title: *Who Knew?* It evolved from the surprise and pride the Milford Writers experienced producing their work.

Who Knew?

Note: each writer has taken responsibility for their editing.

Susan McCoy

Creativity Coach

smccoy68@yahoo.com   www.susanmccoy.blogspot.com

Table of Contents

Barbara Armstrong

TABLE OF CONTENTS

Acknowledgments

Many thanks to Nancy, Director of Milford Senior Center, for urging me to register for my first Creative Writing class. Thank you also to Susan, our resourceful and dedicated teacher who offered patience and encouragement to my amateur efforts to put words and feelings on paper. Thanks to my editors, Andrea, Melissa, Lori, and Linda who not only edited my work but offered suggestions, did multiple readings and also much typing. Thanks to my son and daughter-in-law Bill and Penny for supporting me long distance by phone and email. This has been a wonderful experience and a great opportunity to record some of the many stories of my life.

Biography

Barbara Armstrong grew up in Detroit, Michigan in a family of ten. She has been an avid reader since childhood. Her first writing experience started in college when she enrolled in a creative writing class as a substitute for a required class that was not available that semester. She loved it and set a goal of keeping a journal. After two weeks of journaling her time and enthusiasm waned. After her husband's death she enrolled in a writing class at the senior center. It has help her immensely in the grief process. She has three children living active lives and who have given much support. Ten years ago she moved to the enchanted Village of Milford, Michigan where she is living with her daughter and three cats.

NEW BEGINNINGS

My Lunar Eclipse

In my life there has been someone or something that has been there in times of trouble to guide me and bring relief. My family and friends have been kind and supportive, yet I longed for that special gift. My faith was failing me.

Then last Tuesday morning at 6:00 AM, my daughter came into my bedroom and asked me if I wanted to watch the lunar eclipse. I got up, put on my robe and slippers and went out of the room, the best place to view it. She had set her alarm for 5:30 and was really excited. She didn't want to miss anything.

It was the first lunar eclipse I had ever seen and as I watched I began to think about how it reminded of what was taking place in my life. The moon was full and very bright and as I watched the sun began to cover it very slowly. It was becoming very dark. Almost immediately it reversed and started to uncover the moon. The moon became its bright full self again and then turned a brilliant red. It was a beautiful sight.

My husband had died a few months before and the dark moon reminded me of the dark days I had been through. As it brightened I thought of how my grief was slowly getting easier to manage. My life was adjusting to my loss and I was beginning to think of him and his love, laughter and the joy he gave me and all the good times we had. It's still hard, but now I look up to the sky at night and see the moon and think of him as a bright star watching over me.

Living a More Serene Life, I Hope

Between working, taking care of my husband Bob and running the house, days were sometimes very hectic. Now I'm beginning to realize that it's time to organize and de-clutter. I remember when my sisters and I cleaned out my mother's possessions when she moved to a nursing home. So many things she had loved. Making those decisions of what to keep, what to distribute to us, her children and what to give away was one of the worst times of my life. Many books have been written on the subject of de-cluttering and I had just read one. It was on the best seller list and now the same author has written a new book on packing your suitcase for different occasions. That's on the best seller list too. So apparently I have a lot of company. I want to spare my children the difficult decisions my sisters and I had to make.

I started with my bedroom with the premise that I would be needing someplace to sort out books, records, letters, cards, clothes and my biggest problem, photos. After it was cleaned out, I was tempted to stop my project. It looked so beautiful even my daughter complemented me on its beauty. I made a pact with myself to finish the de-cluttering I had started.

I am now on the next phase of my journey. That's what this is, a big journey that I now realize is going to take a long, long time.

As of this day, March 29, 2016, my bedroom is finished, and most of my walk-in closet is uncluttered. Next, to the pantry, the most cluttered area in the house. There are six piles that I have to tackle, one by one, and about another six piles still in the closet, but the closet is looking better. As for the once beautiful bedroom, need I say more? According to the book, I am supposed to feel joyful and I am.

I guess?

America the Beautiful

I sometimes wish our National Anthem was "America the Beautiful". To me its words typify our country and it sure is much easier to sing!

Oh Beautiful for Spacious Skies

For Amber Waves of Grain

For Purple Mountain Majesties

Above the Fruited Plain!

America, America, God Shed His Grace on Thee

And Crown Thy Good With Brotherhood

From Sea to Shining Sea!

These were my initial thoughts sitting on the train on the first lap of a trip to visit my brother in Oregon. I could not tear my eyes away from the scenes passing by. I had boarded the train in Ann Arbor, Michigan, on my way to Chicago, a three and a half hour trip. I brought my knitting, puzzles, my sketch book and a good novel to read and to ease my boredom on this long trip. Instead my eyes were glued to the window and that is where they stayed.

We made five stops in Michigan to pick up or leave off passengers. I'm very interested in architecture and the old train station in each town usually has a distinct architectural style, unique, quaint, and really lovely. Most of them are not used by the trains anymore, but I hope they will be preserved. After this trip, I would like to do some research about their origins and architects. There must be a book or two devoted to the styles of old train stations.

This trip to Chicago was during a snow storm. Everything was white. It was beautiful and pristine, but the city looked abandoned. As we approached the city, it took on a whole new life. Lake Michigan came into my view twice and all the many condos and marinas surrounding it. Although still empty of people and boats in the winter, soon it would be coming alive for the summer.

Next, the industrial section was before me. The train came to a slowed pace and the buildings looked abandoned and grotesque. However, they still showed evidence of what was a busy and vital city in days gone by.

As the skyline of Chicago came into view, we pulled into the station, dark, full of train tracks, people bustling, gathering their belongings, the conductor giving instructions.

We were hurried into the station by a red cap to a lovely lounge to await the next step of our journey. It would be a three-hour wait until the train departed for Portland, Oregon.

ARCHIVES AND ADVENTURES

Timbertoes

My brother enlisted in the Navy when he graduated from high school to avoid being drafted. We were surprised because he had never shown an interest in boats or the water. After the war, he went to college at night and got a job with an advertising firm. He married, bought a home, had three children and seemed to be settled and happy. Sometime during this period, he acquired the nickname Spike.

Then to our surprise, he bought a small boat and motor. Soon, he graduated to a larger boat and motor and spent his leisure time exploring the small lakes and rivers in southeast Michigan. He seemed to be content just exploring by himself or with his family, never dreaming he had much greater ambitions.

This was when Timbertoes (means man with a wooden leg) made her appearance. She was an offshore sailing and racing boat, built in 1948 and popular in the east coast. He discovered her at the Detroit Yacht Club. She had been neglected forty years and the owners were no longer members of the club. She had sunk and was on the bottom of her 6 foot keel and was a real eyesore at the yacht club in the front docks for all to see. She was a wooden boat and had a 9,000 pound chunk of lead at the bottom of her keel. Overall she weighed 20,000 pounds.

Her original name was Endeavor and she was a 42 foot 7/8 sloop rigged wooden sailboat built by Hinckley Yard in Maine. Spike did extensive research trying to establish her origins to no avail. Her original owners had moved and the club knew little else. He bought the boat for the amount of money the yacht club deemed reasonable just to have the boat removed from the premises. They even graciously threw in a slip in the back of the club (where she would not be seen) to work on the restoration.

Pumping her out took a full day plus she leaked heavily due to rotting timbers and she had to be patched. That was when family members became involved. Relatives and friends came out of the woodwork. We even had a nephew we hadn't seen in years come down from North Dakota and joined in the fun. We scraped, sanded and painted all day and many nights by floodlights. My husband Bob and brother Dick aided in refurbishing the mahogany cockpit, a large eight- foot area. The teak decks and mahogany cap rails needed repair. The spar was Sitka Spruce 64 feet in length and 50 feet above the cabin top.

The boat's first trial run revealed that the step of the mast below the cabin needed sister ribs to strengthen it. Out of the water she came again. This time at the Bayview Yacht Club on their elevator, allowing Spike to caulk her properly. The boom was 29 feet long which meant the sail was huge. Besides the main sail, she had one normal one and one storm sail. None of the sails were self-furling. All had to be hanked on in all kinds of weather. The club gave Spike two small spinnakers to train in how to use them. One of them, a light wind blue, filled with water after lowering it and someone yanked it on board and ripped it. Spike remained calm as usual, but his wife Pauline used some blue language when it happened.

Below deck was a galley, main cabin and aft cabin. I loved the galley. It had an ice box, sink, and a two burner stove. It was very compact so you could just stand in one spot and cook a whole meal. It had all kinds of storage tucked away under the floor planks of the main deck for wine, sodas, veggies and canned goods. The lamps were all gimbaled oil lamps. The head did not have a holding tank and once it got plugged and exploded in Spike's face!

The sink had hot and cold running water. The water was heated by passing over the engine or heated on the stove. On sailing trips, the shower was a large plastic container of water hooked up to the boom over the cockpit and heated by the sun. A hose with a shower head was attached. Privacy was scarce.

Timbertoes had a 29 horsepower motor just to enable it to get in and out of moorings. After night sails going back to the club, down the Detroit River, we had to turn sharply in front of the Roostertail nightclub, drop the sails quickly and start the engine to get into the lagoon. A sight that often drew sighs of relief from the nightclubbing set because it looked like we were going to hit the dock.

Most of our sailing was on Lake St. Clair and Lake Erie and eventually up the Canadian coast, Georgian Bay and the North Channel. Timbertoes was built for offshore ocean sailing and racing so she carried two huge tanks of water under the two main bunks in the main cabin, each holding 150 gallons. When she ran out of water, we filled the tanks with fresh water with a garden hose at the club.

I loved to sleep on the boat looking up at the sky filled with stars and the steady rock and roll of the boat rocking us to sleep. Waking up at first light, having a cup of coffee, then crawling back into the sleeping bag to dream until Spike got up and started the day's chores.

Quite often our three cats sailed with us; Mylai and Freebie, both Siamese, and Peter, a huge black shorthair. Occasionally, our two labs would also sail with us. The dogs would jump ship with the cats to explore the docks, but came bounding back to Timbertoes when we pulled up the anchor.

All these details of Timbertoes were shared with me by my sister-in-law, Pauline. She had many more stories to share with me. I'm looking forward to a sunny, snowy day we can spent together to relive our Timbertoes adventures.

Sailing With "Timbertoes"

My brother's sailboat "Timbertoes" is long gone and so is my brother. He put it up for sale when he was diagnosed with cancer. I asked my sister-in-law Pauline if she had any idea where it was. She said she didn't know who purchased the boat or where the boat was. She told me somebody asked her if she missed sailing and she said she didn't. That was part of her life that she had enjoyed with my brother Spike and that part was over. She still has the kennel and six female labs that she cares for and breeds. They built the kennel to breed Labrador Retrieves and they have been very successful. One of their dogs won Best of Breed at the Westminster Dog Show. She has six females which she breeds and raises until they can be adopted. Her dogs are much in demand.

Pauline did relate to me a couple of interesting stories that happened while on sailing trips. One summer while she was off from her teaching job and Spike was between jobs, they decided to sail the entire summer. The stayed mostly in the North Channel of Georgian Bay in Canada and enjoyed pretty good weather. One evening a young man and his blind date rowed alongside while they were anchored in the bay. He was rowing backwards taking in water and was about to go down when Spike pulled him and his date aboard to dry off.

Spike rescued the dinghy and emptied it of water and tied it off the stern. They soon discovered that the young man had borrowed it from the shore not knowing it belonged to a power boater. Before too long, the owner of the dinghy arrived with the local sheriff to claim the dinghy. Spike and Pauline had hidden the young man and his date below deck so that they would not be arrested. Spike claimed the dinghy had floated by and he was going to turn it in the next morning after the fireworks that evening. The owner of the dinghy and sheriff were reassured and left.

Pauline fixed dinner for the four of them. When it was time to turn in they loaded the cockpit with bags of sails and gave the couple two sleeping bags and that's where they stayed for the night.

The next morning when they weighed anchor and took the couple to the dock, they realized that their friends had left them behind, so they had to rent a car to get back to town. The couple did show their appreciation by buying Pauline and Spike a bag of groceries and some nice steaks to grill later on for dinner. They heard from the young woman a week later. She apologized again for her date's actions. It was their first date and she guessed he was trying to impress her, but failed. She said she was never going to see him again!!!

Partying on Timbertoes

Our adventures on Timbertoes began as soon as the restoration was complete. We ran into problems off and on, but Spike managed to handle every problem, calmly as usual, and got it fixed.

One of our best parties started the eve of the Mackinaw Race weekend. There was always a big crowd of crew members, family and friends, eating, drinking, and celebrating. One of our friends played the guitar and serenaded the crowd. I worried about how they were going to be able to get some sleep before the morning start of the race, but when they appeared on deck to ready the boat for the race, it was all business like any other departure. Spike ran a tight ship and although he never won the race, he made a good showing. Always calm and focused.

One summer, Spike and Pauline invited all the adults in the family for a cruise on Lake St. Clair to celebrate our sisters' birthdays. The sailing at the beginning of the evening was fairly smooth and pleasant, the water calm, the breezes soft. We took turns at the tiller. My brothers all went swimming in their undershorts, diving off the boat. We were having a great time.

All of a sudden, the sky darkened, the wind picked up, the waves got bigger. The boat began to roll, the sails started flapping, lightning lit the sky, thunder roared, a real summer thunder storm.

The captain, Spike, ordered all the women, except Pauline, below deck. The men stayed on deck, helping with the sails and tiller. Spike remained calm and in control. I was a nervous wreck and saying my prayers. Every once in a while, Spike or Pauline would come down to assure us that everything was fine, in control, "just a little storm, be over in a short time". Although I did remember Pauline telling me that on some of their sailing trips, she was saying her rosary and also using some blue language.

Soon the storm turned into a soft rain. The boat stopped rolling and we continued our partying, but in a much more somber mood.

I have many photos of our Timbertoes adventures. I bring them out to look at occasionally and show my grandchildren.

OUR FURRY FAMILY

Our Cats

When we moved into our condo, we had three cats. Lilly and Rosebud are mine, Precious was my daughter Andrea's. Since then, Precious has passed away to be replaced by Annie. Five females living in one house is a bit much.

The restrictions in our condo rules limit residents to one pet. So whenever we receive a visit by a neighbor, we have designated Lilly as our one pet, and if questioned, her name becomes a combined Lillyannrose. Our cats are indoor cats and are afraid of the wild, outside world, except for Lilly who is an escape artist, streaking out every opportunity she gets. When she was younger, it was a problem chasing after her and luring her in with food. But now she is 16 years old, weighty and has an arthritic front paw. We can outrun her!

Rosebud is 20 years old, a survivor. We found her living in a car at a flea market. Her owner was a young lady whose boyfriend hated cats. Consequently, she took the cat with her everywhere.
We had seen the cat sitting in the rear window and when the girl parked, we asked her about the cat. She told us her story and to our surprise she asked, "Do you want her?" We had just lost Precious so we thought for a few minutes and said, "sure" and moved the cat, her bed, food and toys into our car and went on with our day.

She is a Siamese with a black mask on her face, resembling a raccoon. She is shy and not at all friendly with the other two cats. In fact, after many years together, they still hate each other.

Lilly is a big Abyssinian. Each hair on her body is brown, black and white. She is THE alpha cat and rules the other cats and us. She is sixteen years old, is very social and requires a great deal of attention. If she sees one of the other cats favoring something, it then becomes her favorite toy or resting spot. She is very jealous, has to be fed first and rubbed the most.

Annie is our youngest cat, eight years old, a Calico, very pretty tri-color markings. We found out later that all Calicos are female. She is all cat! She chases her tail, is extremely independent and hates to be picked up. Everything on her terms is her personality. After five years of residence, she is just beginning to come out of her shell. She sits for hours in front of the windows, with the shades down. We haven't figured that one out yet.

We love all of our cats but I would love to adopt a dog. A dog would be more of a companion for me. I love to walk and a dog needs to walk, but I hesitate to get one because the cats' noses would be put out of joint for sure.

Rose and Lilly are old and probably won't live too much longer. I hate to think of losing them, so I'll bide my time and practice my dog skills on my daughter Melissa's dog, Dingo, the counter surfer.

The Adoption

Our family always had a cat or two as pets. Most of them were strays, donations from friends or relatives whose own cat had kittens they couldn't keep and begged us to adopt.

Our most unusual adoption involved my aunt Emmie and her two women friends who were psychiatrists. Aunt Emmie was one of my mother's six sisters. We always thought she was a bit flaky but we loved her most of all the sisters. Her stories were hilarious and made us laugh and we always looked forward to her visits.

One afternoon, she called to ask my mother if we would be interested in adopting a kitten that needed a home. Seeing as we were a family that took in aunts, uncles, cousins, grandfathers, and all sorts of animals, cats, dogs, even a duck that shadowed my brother one whole summer. Of course, my mother said, "sure". An appointment was made for the following evening. The owners turned out to be two lovely ladies, quite stern appearing, with a mission in mind. They proceeded to introduce themselves and then, very formally, to the little kitten who was in a box filled with a blanket and a few toys. It was a black and white kitten and cute as could be. Right then, we knew it would be ours.

Before the ladies would leave the kitten with us, however, they were very firm that they be sure the kitten was comfortable in our home and would cause no trouble for us.

They took some time selecting where its bed and food dish should be placed and then its litter box location to avoid any accidents. They proceeded to take the kitten to the sink and hold it near the running water, and then they put it in its new litter box, gently coaxing the kitten to use the box. They kept on doing this for three or more trips. We were standing there watching this whole procedure fascinated. Amazingly, the kitten complied by urinating in the box and covering it up with its little paws. Satisfied and happy that the kitten was going to love its new home and no trouble to us they graciously thanked us and left. That was my first experience with psychology!

CRUISING ALONG

And I Got To Pick The Color

I was having a day of writers block. I soon picked up my book "Families Writing" and followed a suggestion they had, cars that you owned. It turned out to be a great experience! It brought back so many happy memories. Many times as I was writing, I burst out laughing. Cars and driving them were such a great part of our lives as a family. Here is a list of some of those happy times.

1936 Black Ford Sedan that my husband Bob borrowed from his brother along with $75.00 for our honeymoon trip to Niagara Falls. At the stop for the border with Canada, the inspector looked at us, then at the car and said, "On your honeymoon? Hope you make it back home." We not only made it home, but went by way of Cleveland! Love conquers all!

A 1948 Chevrolet Bel-air Coupe.
The first car Bob and I owned. I was working at Fisher Body in the Time Study Office. Executives of the company brought their new cars into the factory outside the office to have their cars customized. One of the executives was selling his son's car. It was silver with a red interior. We had been tooling around on a motorcycle that Bob bought when he came home from the service. We sold the motorcycle for $500.00 and bought the car.

A 1952 Karmann Ghia. Bob was stationed in Germany for two years and fell in love with the design of foreign cars. It was a two-seater with a fold-down back seat that served as a large padded surface for the kids to play and sleep. There were no car seat requirements then! I drove it to my driver's license test with my small baby daughter sleeping in the back. Bob offered to take her with him but the policeman insisted we not wake her. Halfway through the test, she woke and started to cry. The test was cut short. Four right turns back to the station then pulled over to the curb. I got my license! I was seven months pregnant when Bob invited his mother to go for a drive in his new sport car. He seated her in the front seat, me in the cramped back seat, my stomach hitting my chin. I began to think that baby was going to be born right then! That was the era of the bullet rear end Cadillac and they were forever backing up into our slick little Karmann Ghia. One time we went to a movie in Detroit. When we returned to our car, some jokesters had picked it up and planted it on the sidewalk. Needless to say we didn't keep that car very long.

A 1954 Putrid Green Four-Door Fiat Sedan, our next foreign car.
Bob had ordered a British car to be delivered in a few weeks. We waited and waited for it. Finally, after a few months, we confronted the salesman. He informed us that the delivery was delayed because they had to reorder it as the original car had fallen off the boat on its trip to America. We decided to change our source for cars.

We drove the Fiat for many years until Bob got a new job that came with a new car every two years. We lived in the suburbs and I had never had a car at my disposal unless I drove Bob to work in the morning with three kids half asleep. The Fiat would become mine! I was deliriously happy for a few days. Driving it home from work one day, he came into the house and his first words were, "There goes your car". "What do you mean" I asked. His answer was "The gas tank fell off down the road and it would be too expensive to fix it." I'm a quiet, reserved person normally but that ended right there. The car was repaired. I drove it and our children around for the next two or three years after that.

A 1962 Silver Four-Door Buick Special with a bright red interior.

The Fiat was our last foreign car. Bob decided foreign cars were too expensive to repair. The Buick was one of my favorite cars and we drove it to the ground. It took us on many of our adventures. Bob loved to drive. The only problem was he hated to stop and always got sleepy during the day but not at night. We packed a small cooler with noisy chewing food to keep him awake. We took turns keeping a vigil to feed him to keep him awake. Also, pit stops were a problem. The children had to start crying before he found it necessary to pull into a rest stop. We drove that car to Winnipeg, Canada on a camping trip that Bob insisted was only going to take a two-day drive but turned into five days. Fortunately, it was one of our longest vacations and we had a great time. When we ask our children what their favorite vacation was, the answer is Winnipeg. When the Buick was ten years old, we drove it to the airport, stopped to get gas and the attendant asked if he could buy it. We were amazed! We sold it to him the next day. That car had a long history in our lives.

About then, Bob got a job that came with a car every two years (or 45,000 miles), after which he got a new car and I got the old one. Sometimes they came with minor or major problems that required repairs but Bob was always reluctant to spend money on them and I was too happy to have a car of my own to complain about.

A 1964 Four-Door Green Ford Sedan - our first company car.
Bob hated the color but he had no choice - it was the last car available. We always called it the "Green Pea" when referring to it. I don't remember too much about our experiences driving it. I do know that we were very happy when the two years were up.

A 1965 Four-Door Dark Blue Oldsmobile Sedan - We loved this car!
We drove it for two happy years. It was big and roomy, ideal for two adults and three growing children. We had started going on long camping trips and needed room for all of our camping equipment. When the time came to give it up we decided to keep it and it became my car to drive to my first job.

A 1967 Two-Door Dark Green Plymouth Barracuda - I got to pick out the color for this car.
We drove this car to the Expo 67 in Montreal, Canada. Bob's brother and his family flew to Michigan from California to go with us and drove our Oldsmobile while we drove the Barracuda to Montreal. There were eleven of us including my mother-in-law who decided at the last minute to go with us. I rented a house in Montreal to eat breakfast and sleep in. The rest of the day we were at Expo.

It was very crowded and we had a terrible time keeping track of our group but we had a ball. The best part was that the cousins got to spend time together! My son Bill learned to drive in this car. He wasn't into maintenance, just gas, and drove it without oil one night and wrecked the engine. We had it repaired at a great expense and kept it for a long time.

A 1970 Two-Door Copper Pontiac T-37 Sedan - Our most beautiful car. We loved it and so did everyone else. My daughter Andrea learned to drive with this car with Bob as her teacher. It did not go very well, especially with Andrea. She came home and complained that her Dad would not answer her questions. He would just say "What do you think?" She has turned out to be an excellent driver with a perfect record. This car became my next car and I drove it for years. It is now a collector's car. We see it often in the Woodward Dream Cruise in Michigan.
Since then, we have driven two GMC Safari Vans which carried our bicycles to all of our touring events all over the country and to Canada.

I eventually purchased my own car, a Silver Nissan 240 sports car with a manual transmission. I fell in love with it in the showroom on my lunch hour, went back to work and announced that was the car for me. I had learned to drive on cars with manual transmissions, but that was a while before, so I had to learn all over again. I didn't realize until my first hard winter that it was a rear-wheel drive vehicle and didn't do well on snowy days even with snow tires. I kept it for several years and eventually traded it in for a Honda Element, the exact opposite style of car. It offered theatre-type viewing in the back seating area so Bob, who had stopped driving, had good visibility on our long ride.

That's the long history of our love of cars and driving. Our favorite pastime is to go for long drives, exploring the countryside. We always lived on the east side of Detroit so when we moved to Milford, Michigan, we had much exploring to do. Our friends think we are crazy! It's nothing for us to take off on a sunny day and drive aimlessly through the countryside, exploring small towns, markets, gardens and especially, hardware stores and interesting architecture.

Our children share the same delight in exploring by car but not our grandchildren! They are bored and require entertainment. We actually rented a TV for the car so our granddaughter could be entertained on a long trip. Car games didn't do it for her or them.

FAMILY TIES

The Picnic That Wasn't a Picnic For Me

Our family met at a local lake most summers for a reunion. It included my mom and dad and most of my siblings (there were ten of us), my mother's six sisters and two brothers and assorted cousins. It was an all-day event with plenty of food, games, swimming and much laughter. My two uncles were comedians, keeping us in stitches much of the time. It was the only time we saw these relatives each year unless there was a wedding or funeral in the family. The adults usually sat around the picnic table talking, eating and catching up on the latest gossip. The children wore bathing suits and immediately took to the water. Somebody usually brought two or three black inner tubes to float on. Seeing as there were about six to eight children, we all hoped to get at least one turn on one of them. I was about seven or eight that year and the only girl. The only other girl was a cousin who was fifteen and she had brought her boyfriend and they took off immediately to be alone.

The boys dominated the tubes, having fun jumping on and off, splashing and fighting over them. My chances seemed slim for ever having a turn on the tubes. I got impatient and decided the only way I was going to get a tube was to enter the fray. After many failures, I managed to grab one, jump on it and paddle away furiously to get as far away from the boys as I could. It was my turn! They soon lost interest and started playing on the other tubes.

It wasn't long before I realized that I had left the boys far behind. I could hardly make them out in the water anymore. I was safe at last! I relaxed and felt the water drifting me along, just enjoying myself with my hands in the water paddling leisurely. I felt pretty smug watching them from afar.

It wasn't long before I was bored and decided to start back. It was lonely out there and I was missing the fun. I decided not to go directly but veered off to the side. I wanted to surprise them. After a while I saw a small dock, a perfect place to get off the tube and casually walk back with the tube. As soon as I reached the dock, I jumped off the tube expecting to touch the bottom. Instead of feeling the bottom right away, I kept going down. The water got murky and I felt weeds brushing against my legs. It wasn't shallow, it was deep. I panicked! I began thrashing the water with my arms and kicking. I couldn't think. I began to rise, swallowing water as I went up. My head cleared the water. I was gasping for air and starting to go down again. Suddenly, I felt someone grab me, lifting me out of the water, and firmly set me back onto the tube. It was a man. I hadn't seen another person while I was in the water around me. Nobody. He gave the tube a little push and said in a quiet voice "Don't ever do that again" then he disappeared. I was so frightened!

I slowly paddled back to shore, got out of the tube. One of the boys grabbed the tube, didn't ask any questions, then took off with it as if nothing happened. It hadn't, for him. I walked to the picnic table where my parents sat. I was trembling. No one noticed. They were busy in their conversations. I grabbed a towel, wrapped it around me. No one knew what had happened and I didn't say a word. I thought if I told someone, I would be in trouble. After a while, I began looking toward the water where I had been on the tube. I saw nobody. I looked all over the beach at the other picnickers. I thought he was probably watching me to see what I did, if I was safe, but nobody showed any interest. I was silent the rest of the day and never went back into the water.

Until I wrote this story, I have never told a single person about this experience, but I will not swim anywhere unless I can feel the bottom of the water. I am strictly a pool swimmer. I'm afraid my rescuer will not be there.

Piecing Our Lives Together

My mother Mary and mother-in-law Minnie both pieced together quilts, but for different reasons and used entirely different techniques.

My mother's quilts were strictly for practical purposes. We had a large family and our bedrooms were on the second floor and not very warm during the winter months. In fact, we woke up in the morning and Jack Frost had painted our windows with lovely designs, which we loved.

My mother's quilts were always squares cut from our old clothes. She used our sewing machine to stitch them together. The fillings were usually old quilts or blankets resulting in a very heavy quilt that weighed us down. The backing was always new fabric with a print suited to our tastes. The colors of the patches weren't necessarily coordinated but we identified the squares that were from our clothes - who wore them when and where. It always brought up many memories and stories and kept us amused when we were sick and couldn't go to school.

Minnie's quilts were much more decorative and all hand sewn. She sent for the patterns from the newspaper. She had dozens of them and all had names like "star quilt", "double wedding ring" quilt and so on. She cut out the different pieces and colors and pinned all the pieces together that became a square. She did all the piecing in the warm summer months.

The squares were joined together to form the front of the quilt. The backing was a solid material and color that coordinated with the front of the quilt.

During the winter months, the quilting began. She used large wooden hoops and sat in her chair with the quilt spread out over her lap. This kept her warm and cozy while she quilted and watched "I Love Lucy", "The Jack Benny Show", and in later years "The Mary Tyler Moore Show".

When the quilts were finished, the backing was as beautiful as the patchwork pattern on the front. It was a shame not to see the small stitches that formed a beautiful pattern. Sometimes I make the bed with the back showing and marvel at the intricacy of the pattern.

After Bob and I were married and had children, I would supply Minnie with all the remnants from sewing my own and my children's clothes.

After each quilt was finished, she carefully folded them up, put them in plastic bags and stored them under her bed. She usually finished two each winter and it got pretty crowded. As her children and grandchildren married, her gifts to them was one of her quilts.

I have two twin quilts pieced together from scraps of my daughters' dresses, pajamas, pants and tops. I use them as bedspreads and my daughters loved to tell stories about them to their sleep-over friends.

One of the most elaborate quilts is pieced together from tiny pieces of delicate shades of yellow and other pastel prints that form intertwining rings. It is called a "double wedding ring" pattern. It is very large and the edges are all scallops. I only use it on special occasions.

Another of our quilts was lost. Our son Bill begged to borrow it for a play as a prop. I resisted, but he promised to bring it home after the play. I gave in. I never saw the quilt again. I can still see that green and white quilt and hope that someone is treasuring it as we did.

Another quilt made by Bob's grandmother of wool men's suit pieces put out a small fire in our home, but that's another story.

Minnie lived to be 93 years old. When we were clearing out her house, we found ten quilts under her bed, all finished, folded perfectly and in their plastic bags. Now they are wedding gifts for her great grandchildren.

My mother lived to be 90. We still use her quilts. They are indestructible. We keep one in our car all the time. Another one is our picnic quilt.

All of these quilts have had a major part of keeping our families together over the years. They remind us of our mothers' love and the happy times we have had together.

Driving Miss Bonnie

What is that saying "The best laid plans go astray". Well, that's what happened when my siblings and I decided to take our 95- year- old sister, Bonnie shopping at Meijer. She had painstakingly made a list of 15 items she needed. Maryann, my other sister, got to the nursing home early to sort out the items on the list. Many items she already had but couldn't find, so a new list was made. When I got there, both sisters were all ready to go. Bonnie was in her best outfit, hair professionally done and acting very impatient!

The first hurdle was getting her into a transfer chair from the bulky hospital wheelchair and into the car. We were informed that we needed permission to do this transfer which took a while. Finally, mission accomplished and we got her into the car with a great deal of help from the staff. That was when it dawned on us, there were five of us with my brother-in-law John, the driver, my brother Emile, visiting from Eugene, Oregon, myself, my sister Maryann plus Bonnie going on this shopping trip in a compact sedan. After much laughter and maneuvering three adults squeezed into the back seat.

Maryann had gotten some instructions from Bonnie's son about how to get to the store as none of us had been there before, but with a few detours we found it.

By now, a considerable amount of time had passed and if we were going to get the shopping done, have lunch and get back to the nursing home for our next appointment on time; we had about two hours left. Another hurdle! Right then we planned that we would have to divide up at the store each with a different shopping goal. Maryann would get the underwear, John would find a hairnet (never found), and comb. I would take Bonnie with me to select pants and matching top. Bonnie had difficulty deciding on the outfit but with a little pressure from me she selected something that pleased her. The shopping was finished in record time.

On to our next hurdle, lunch. All trips with Bonnie MUST include lunch, preferably at a very nice restaurant. Looking at my watch, it had to be someplace close and fast. Holding my breath, I suggested "Meijer". We only had an hour left to eat and get back to the nursing home, get Bonnie out of the car, into her room, settled, without seeming to be rushed. Bonnie didn't bat an eyelash and said Meijer was fine. We proceeded to the food service area, selected a few entrees and beverages, popped them in the microwave oven, found a table and gobbled down our lunch. Through all this rushing, Bonnie was completely calm and unaware. I started laughing hysterically. I was having a really hard time controlling myself. It was contagious, because everybody else starting laughing, too.

We made it! We arrived back at the nursing home only 10 minutes late with Bonnie happy and content. The rest of us were tired but ready for our next appointment.

The next day, Monday, my brother visiting from Oregon and I went for a walk in town. As we were walking, my brother saw a sign in the window of a restaurant advertising a big assortment of pies. "How would you like a pie lunch", he asked me. "I'd love it", I said. After our pie and tea lunch, as we were walking out the door, a big curly coated red dog blocked our way looking like he was coming into the restaurant. We were startled when a woman suddenly pulled him back. As she did, I looked beyond him and saw a woman in a wheelchair. At first, I didn't recognize her. Another look, and then I did. It was my sister, Bonnie, all dressed up in her new outfit, probably wearing her new underwear, with a new entourage going out for a stroll and lunch!!!

Christmas

In the December 24th Detroit News Think section, there was an article by Garrison Keillor called 'You Don't Have to Believe to Believe in Christmas". I read it and thought about Christmas in my family. It has always been an important holiday for us. We always had a big tree, decorated it, and stashed our gifts under it on Christmas Eve. We would move the sofa into the dining room to make room for the tree. On Christmas Eve, I stayed up most of the night to keep the tree "company". I still keep that tradition in my own home when I can. There were ten children in our family, five boys and five girls. If a child was sick at Christmas time, and there usually was at least one ill child every Christmas, she or he slept on the sofa to be near my parent's bedroom so my mother could care for him or her. When my brother came home after a long stint in the army, everything related to family, especially the holidays, were very important to him. His first Christmas home, he spent hours hanging silver foil icicles meticulously on every branch of the tree.

Even though times were hard, we bought or made gifts for everyone. I remember embroidering pillow cases, towels, tablecloths and napkins and selling them to my relatives. One Christmas, my oldest brother sent me two classic Louisa May Alcott books, "Little Women" and "Eight Cousins" from Germany. I still have them. We always went to church at midnight to listen to the Christmas story and music.

I could go on and on about what Christmas means to me, but as I was going through the newspapers last week and came upon Garrison Keillor's article, I sat down and read it. I do believe in Christmas but I know some don't. My sister has been in a nursing home for four years now. Her family doesn't believe in Christmas but I know she does. So we take her gifts, decorate her room, visit her.

This is our second Christmas without my husband Bob. It was easier than last year. Hopefully as time goes by, Christmas will become more of a celebration with less sadness. I will never want to not celebrate the holidays: outdoor decorations and lights, the tree, the family get-togethers, our friends visiting, the gift giving and receiving.

It's now a month past Christmas and our tree is still up. Come February, we will remove the Christmas ornaments and fill the tree with hearts of all kinds. It is a tradition we started a few years ago, a "Valentines Tree" and now some of our friends are following this tradition too.

Marnie Dooling

.

~ Musings ~

By Marnie

I dedicate this book to my mother,

Frances M. Emblin (Mills)

Who gave me life,

Was unselfish in her desires,

Understanding in all my problems,

Unnerving in her Christian devotion, and

Absolutely my best friend.

Many thanks go out to my daughter,

Deborah Danko

Who poured over and through this work

Offering suggestions and corrections,

And for providing essential word processing

And technical support.

February 17, 2007

Dear Mom & Dad,

As I was traveling back to California from Grandma Rhoten's funeral, a very important thought struck me...like a ton of bricks. Relationships don't just happen.

I want to say THANK YOU for keeping us in touch all these years with the Rhoten side of the family. Not all parents would have done what you did, schlepping us back and forth each year for Easter and other events. It might have been easy to have let those Ohio relationships slip away over the years.

Our family is exceptionally close. I know too many people who haven't spoken to a family member for years or even decades. We are close because of you guys...the way you brought us up.

Thank you for doing such a great job at molding us into the great people we are today.

Anyway, I just wanted to let you know that what you did, whether intentional or not, didn't go unnoticed or unappreciated.

I know my siblings feel the same way.

Love you,

Deb

(Letter written to me by my daughter, Deborah Danko, following her grandmother's funeral in Ohio)

About the Author

Marlene F. Dooling, age 81 of Milford, Michigan is the author of the "Musings by Marnie" section of this book. Most of the stories in the book are about Marnie or her family.

Born in Detroit of Fred and Frances Emblin, Marnie was raised in Michigan, and graduated from Berkley High School in 1953. Marlene married Don Rhoten in 1955 and had four children: Deborah K. Danko, Kimberly J. Dangleis, Cynthia M. Curry, and Donald D. Rhoten Jr. Don (senior) died in a tragic car accident in August 1965. Marnie married John J. Dooling in September 1967. Together, they have one son, John J. Dooling Jr.

Marnie also has 6 grandchildren and 6 great-grandchildren. Her sister Cristie lives in San Jose with her family.

Hobbies enjoyed by Marnie include golf (Ladies Golf Champion Highland Hills), playing poker and bridge, painting and ceramics. She is a member of the Red Hat Society and is a Daughter of the American Revolution (DAR) active member.

Marnie's interests have come full circle. Beginning with creative arts in high school, she enjoyed painting, chalk drawing, designing and tooling leather purses, and fashion sewing. After her kids were all in school, she earned her real estate license. For the next 35 years, Marnie was a Top Producer REALTOR® winning sales awards, took on the role as agent trainer, and ultimately Manager of a large local real estate brokerage. If that wasn't enough, Marnie then steeped herself more in the technical aspects of real estate earning her license as a real estate appraiser.

In 1999, Marnie was diagnosed with Stage IV small cell lung cancer. After a tough battle, and against all odds, Marnie survived and today is considered a "medical miracle." The only residual effects of the multiple rounds of chemotherapy and radiation are that she has lost her sense of smell, and now requires the use of a walker to help maintain her balance. Today, she is back in the creative realm with "Musings by Marnie."

Coat of Arms

Shield Chandler shows Gyronny of six argent and azure:

The one we use has an ermine crest (a mark of great dignity), a demi-lion regarding or girdled between the paws of a mill rind Sable. The mill rind between the paws and the center of the shield represents an instrument fixed in the stone of a mill that holds and guides the millstone in its course.

It is said to be a bearing applicable to Judges, Magistrates, and others who give equal justice to all.

Contents of
Musings by Marnie

~ 1 ~

My Trip Across the United States - 1945

The Second World War was going on; I was young and didn't pay too much attention to the news. But my uncle was in the Army so when he was home he was in uniform. I also remember at Christmas dinner we said a prayer for our cousin who was missing in action. I later learned that my cousin was killed at the "Battle of the Bulge."

After the attack on Pearl Harbor on December 7, 1941 my dad joined the Navy. I was an only child at the time which made it possible for him to be drafted, so he selected the Navy. I believe he joined in March 1942.

Sometime in 1945, my dad's ship was torpedoed and he came home on leave. His ship was the USS Lamberton, a mine sweeper. At that time my mom and dad decided to spend the leave time driving back to California.

We left Detroit and drove to Chicago to pick up a man who was on my dad's ship and his wife. We stayed in a downtown hotel. I amused myself by riding the elevator up and down. I became known to the hotel patrons as the "J.L. Hudson elevator operator". It was the first time I had eaten all my meals, breakfast, lunch and dinners out in restaurants.

There are a few memories that have stayed with me over the years. I remember going over a very large bridge crossing the Mississippi River. I was very frightened and wanted to hide my face, but was stuck sitting in the middle of the seat with nowhere to hide. We also stayed in a Motor Lodge where I recall getting out of the car and walking in "The Great Salt Lake." Then there were the Great Rocky Mountains. It took days to get over and around them.

Along the way we stopped for lunch in Reno, Nevada where I ordered a hot roast beef sandwich. I guess the meat was tough or something, because my dad got mad and said to the waitress "you expect my daughter to eat this? She can't even cut it". I was embarrassed, so I asked to be excused to go to a store around the corner. I don't remember what kind of store it was, or even if I bought anything. What I do remember is getting lost. I must have turned the wrong way coming out of the store because when I came around the corner the restaurant was not there! I must have looked scared and confused because a man in uniform asked what was wrong. I told him I was lost, described the restaurant and told him my mother and dad were waiting for me there. The gentleman said he knew that restaurant, told me to follow him, which I did. My parents were just getting ready to call the police! I am fairly sure I never went anywhere alone the rest of the trip.

We arrived in San Francisco and stayed in a rooming house which was next to a deep canyon where we played. I met some boys over at the canyon. They had tied a thick rope with a large knot on the bottom of it to a tree. We would back up as far as we could, holding the rope, then run and swing out over the canyon. Stopping yourself when swinging back was the tricky part. I was, and probably still am, a tomboy. I loved swinging over that canyon!

One day my dad came home from wherever he had been. He was dressed in his Navy Whites and asked, "What are you doing out here? So I showed him, and took a swing out over the canyon. He surprised us by asking "can I do it?" The boys ask him if he was sure. So off he went, out over the canyon. But on his way back, his legs were too long and he scraped the canyon side, getting his dress whites very dirty. My mother wasn't sure how she was ever going to get his uniform clean!

We then left San Francisco and headed for San Diego where we lived in a Quonset hut for a while. The only thing I remember about this move, besides the hut, was it was my 10th birthday - April 7, 1945. From there we moved into naval housing and I started school. I didn't know anyone, but soon got acquainted with some girls and was allowed to go visit them.

During this time, a few of my dad's Navy buddies would come over. My dad had some great friends that stayed friends even after the war was over. One or two even came to visit with their wives and kids after we moved back to Michigan. I remember one who referred to himself as "West by God Virginia", I didn't know what that meant, so we called him Bud. He came to my wedding. I guess being the only child out there in Navy housing, I became all their daughters.

In August of 1945 my dad's ship was out on maneuvers. On the day his ship was due in, my mother and I, along with her friend who had a baby named P.J. went down to the wharf to meet my dad's ship. When my mother learned his ship was going to be late, she put me on the Coronado Ferry with 9-month old P.J. On the way over to Coronado Island, suddenly all the ships in the harbor, including the one I was on, starting blowing their horns. It was very loud, P.J. was crying, I was scared and wanted to cry. Somebody stopped and asked me who I was with, and I said "no one." He explained to me that the war was declared over, and every ship and everybody was very happy. I was so glad the man took the time to explain to me that I had to finish the ride over to Coronado and wait, not to give up my seat, and after we returned and docked then I could get off.

When we got back, the streets were full of sailors and people were dancing in the streets. My dad's ship came in 4 hours later, BLOWING THEIR HORN!

After my Dad was mustered out, he sold our car and we took the train back to Michigan. We got home early in October and it was back to school for me. Boy, did I have a lot of catching up to do. By the way, I really enjoyed the trip home. I wandered all over the train, and couldn't make any wrong turns and get lost there.

~ 2 ~

Guess What?

I couldn't have guessed in a million years what my mother (who was not in a very good mood at the time) wanted me to guess. The answer was, "You are getting that baby brother or sister you always wanted." I was 14 years old.

The first thing that popped into my mind was a visit to see Santa Clause when I was 5. I had whispered in Santa's ear that I wanted a baby sister (but I told my mother I had asked for a doll). My dad was thrilled. He wanted a boy and had already decided to name him Donald Frederick Emblin. Me, I was concerned that I was going to end up being a full-time babysitter. I was a junior in high school. Not cool.

Before the baby came, the three of us were sitting at the kitchen table having a name debate. The boy name my dad picked was fine with my mother and me. The girl name was up in the air. My mother wanted Christine or Crystal and to call her Christie. But Dad said, "if you're going to call her Christie, then name her Christie."

I am not sure how the spelling of my sister's name ended up Cristie (without the h) Lynn Emblin, but if I had to guess, it would be that my dad got his way and gave the hospital that version of the name for her birth certificate.

When Cristie was born she had wild black hair and arrived home from the hospital wearing a bonnet. For a while, my dad wanted her in a bonnet, particularly when company came over to see her. Anyway she was so cute, I immediately adored her.

When she got a little older, I was dating Don Rhoten at the time. On Friday nights, we would go to the drive-in movie and I usually volunteered to take Cristie with us... (But that is another story in itself.)

The last vacation the four of us took was to Florida. Cristie was a royal pain in my neck and my dad didn't like a fuss, so I usually gave in to her. So, I nicknamed her Queenie.

Fast forward to my wedding rehearsal. Cristie was my flower girl, and as Queenie, she wanted to walk with my dad, who was walking me down the aisle. This time I threw the bloody fit and my mother had to step in. In the end, Cristie walked in front of my dad and me, properly throwing her petals.

After I was married and staying at home with my kids, Cristie would spend the summers with us. There were lots of kids in the area. In fact, that is where she met her future husband who she ultimately married and moved to California.

The fact is, because of the fourteen year age difference, Cristie and I were essentially both "only children".

~ 3 ~

How to Get to Europe on $9.00

When I was 29, my husband Don who worked for Ford Tractor was transferred to south England to set up a plant. The project should have taken three months. Since we had three small children, I stayed behind. But after Don was there for six months, he started to complain to the company. So Ford told him I would be joining him there in three weeks. This would prove to be no small feat.

1st   Apply for a passport.

2nd   Get a clean bill of health and necessary shots.

3rd   Find a babysitter for the girls.

We got paid once a month and I was scheduled to leave 3 days before payday. I had bills to pay, including the mortgage, car payment, and utilities. So I borrowed enough money from my mom and dad to pay the bills and travel to England. Now, I couldn't leave the girls in old jammies, tennies, and undies...what would their grandparents think? When I got done shopping for the kids, I had $9.00 left.

My in-laws dropped me off at the airport, then continued on with the girls to Ohio where they lived. My sister had been staying with me; so she waited at the house for my mother to pick her up. On the way back to her house my mother mused… "I hope Marlene has enough money." Cristie told her I left the country with $9.00, but it was too late to do anything.

My plane stopped in Boston, where I spent $1.00 on a Pepsi. Now I'm down to $8.00.

When I got to Heathrow Airport, there was a man holding a sign with my name on it. He drove me around and gave me the best tour of London including the Windsor Castle, Kensington Castle, Big Ben, and their largest department store. At the end of the day, I offered to tip him (after all, I still had $8.00), but he said "no thanks, I work for Ford." Don and I were staying in South End on Sea.

The next day I learned I was on an expense account for $6.00 per day. Wow!

I took trains, cabs, and the underground tube. I toured everywhere while Don was working. I also became acquainted with four other Ford wives, who had gone nowhere and seen nothing since they arrived. They were thrilled with my curiosity and we had fun together

I finished spending the $8.00 on two kilts and material for the kids (Blackwatch pattern), and a beautiful wool dress for me. I believe Deb still has her kilt.

p.s. Don ended up working in London for 13 months.

Photo from <u>www.pixabay.com</u> free images

~ 4 ~

A Time to be Born, A Time to Die

August 16, 1965, was the day that changed my life forever. I had three children, ages 8, 5 and 2, and was 4 months pregnant.

My husband Don was working overtime at Ford Tractor. When he called that night, he said he was on his way and would bring home White Castle hamburgers for dinner.

Time went by, he was very late, and I finally put the girls to bed. The circumstances were Don was driving south on Dequindre Rd at the same time 3 old ladies were driving west on Thirteen Mile Road. The ladies failed to stop, and hit Don on the driver side door. He was thrown out of the car. The car he was driving was an older model, before seat belts. He was taken to a small Macomb County Hospital, technically DOA.

When the Sterling Heights Police called me to tell me where he was, I asked a few questions and was told he had a broken leg.

My neighbors across the street, Jerry & Rosalie, had come across the accident scene on their way home. They were sitting on their front porch waiting for my phone to ring. When it did, they were instantly at my front door - Jerry offered to drive me to the hospital and Rosalie would stay with the kids.

Thinking Don had only a broken leg I said, "thank you, but when I bring him home, our station wagon would be best."

I had never been to Macomb General Hospital. I came in the Emergency entrance and wandered all over looking for the front desk. When I found the front desk, the nurse had a stack of papers for me to sign. I did not know exactly what I was signing, what to approve, or what not to approve. I asked if I could call my parents who lived 45 minutes away.

After reading the paperwork, it was clear I needed to call Don's mother and dad. They lived in Ohio, a three hour drive away. It was now 10:00 pm.

I paced the halls of the hospital, waiting for news on Don and for family to arrive. In my wanderings, I opened a door and found myself in the very room where the medical teams were working on my husband. Don lived for about 50 hours; code blue was called 5 times.

Donald Dean Rhoten died Monday August 16th, 1965 at the age of 29 years old. Five months later, I delivered our baby boy.

~ 5 ~

"The Shore"

Anyone who identifies with "The Shore" has been to the Atlantic Ocean in New Jersey… not just the beach, or any other fun place on the water, but the Jersey shore.

Every other year, we packed 6 or 7 people in our large station wagon (there were no vans back then), and headed out for our favorite vacation spot. We ate dinner, did the dishes, prepared the kids for bed, and then left for the 12 hour, 700 mile trip. We left at 8:00 pm, drove all night, and hoped the kids slept all the way.

Most trips to "The Shore" were uneventful but for one. On that occasion, in the middle of the night while I was driving the mountains of Pennsylvania, passing a truck uphill in the pouring rain, suddenly my headlights passed over a large object in the middle of the road. It was unavoidable; I hit it and got 2 blowouts.

The car was pulling hard to the left and there was a steep drop-off so I quietly reached over and woke up John and said, "listen to me. We have 2 blown tires and I need you to let me know when I can pull this car over. Then help me with the steering wheel." My new hair-do was about to be ruined and my bladder was full. We pulled over, and John started walking back to find out what I had hit when the State Police pulled up and ask what happened. I told them the story, but their only response was "I doubt that, lady."

Then John came back to the car and asked the police for their help. It took all 3 of them to pull a tractor-trailer-axle off the road.

John had just put 4 new tires on the station wagon. The police officer said he knew a dealer in the next town who would come out in the middle of the night to sell us new tires. So we all got back in the car to wait for our rescue. After about an hour we all went into town to get new tires. All of this, and the dealer only charged $99.00 per tire plus $15.00 for the trip. John gave the dealer a hefty tip and we were on our way.

We always rented in the same New Jersey town, Ocean City, and usually between 45th and 50th Streets. We brought the same beach umbrellas, same beach chairs, and same blankets so that anyone in our family would be able to find us and join us for the day. We loved the years we had John's Dad with us. It was such a bonding time for the whole family.

Through the years we had an ebb and flow of various family members...boyfriends, husbands and wives, my parents, and grandkids.

Our trips sometimes proved to be real-life educational experiences. We were there in Ocean City when "Hurricane Belle" roared up the eastern coastline. That year the kids experienced first-hand what the eye of the Hurricane is. Another time, we got all 5 kids out of bed at 3:30 in the morning to witness history on TV to see the first man walk on the moon.

Years flew by, the kids grew up, got jobs and started families of their own. The station wagon is long gone, but the memories are as fresh as yesterday for everyone.

We visited Ocean City from 1968 through 2005. We all miss our time at "The Shore."

Below is a heartwarming paper written by my daughter, Cindi.

Car trips loom large in our family's history. To Grandmas' house, the shore, skiing, to Schrader's lake and the Sue locks. I think back on the vacations of our youth – the bickering, the singing, the geology lessons and the laughter – and realize that our best anecdotes as an adult come from those childhood excursions.

We listened to static-infused local radio stations, as dad would fiddle with the dial. We would get a pretty strong signal for about 60 miles, then it would falter and the search would begin again. Finally in later years we had a vehicle with an 8-track player and would be forced to listen to the "horsey song." The wagon became a moving classroom. We learned to read maps. We learned about local history and weather systems.

The back of the station wagon was our domain, to be carved into personal spaces to suit our moods. This was before seat belts, when kids would lay in the rear window to toast in the sun and watch the sky, or at night watch "the bombs", which were the reflections of the oncoming traffic headlights. We were free-range passengers, and we made beds in foot wells and forts behind the coolers at the very back of the back. When we tired of the bickering, we would exchange the seat arrangements.

As we grew older, the sniping ceased and the years of helpless, stop or I'll wet my pants laughter followed. There was no one funnier in than we were, we believed, and if something was funny once, well then, it was funny a hundred times as we giggled and snorted our way across America. As for our long suffering parents, usually a reach for the visor with the hidden paddle or the words, "If I have to stop this car…" would put a calm to us.

Though we all eventually went our separate ways, we remain close. I believe this is partly because we were soldered together by miles and miles of shared experience, by slices of summer vacation lived on the road. We rode over the sticky blacktops of Ohio and climbed through the Appalachian Mountains, all the while laughing, singing over bridges and talking over each other. These memories are as fresh as yesterday, and still invoke bursts of laughter at family gatherings.

Love ya all, Cindi

~ 6 ~

My Favorite Three Houses

1 – 26286 Meadowbrook Way, Lathrup Village, MI

John and I selected the lot and a builder in 1969. This was our first house. A beautiful 4 bedroom, 2 ½ bath with den, living room, formal dining room, kitchen, family room, finished basement, and a screened-in porch. We later had to add a swimming pool.

The reason we had to put in the pool was this: one year we went up north to buy a cabin. We rented a cabin and a boat for two weeks to try it out. But by the end of the trip, no one ever used the boat, there was no phone or TV, no one liked to fish, or wanted to learn to water ski. The kids didn't like any of the restaurants. We spent two weeks with miserable teenagers. So we decided to put in the pool, and everyone was happy.

LARGE PIE-SHAPED LOT enhances this handsome Lathrup Village home. Center-Pass hall, family room, 4 bedrooms, 2½ baths, porch and completely mainte-nance free, in-ground pool with solar cover. Privacy.

We raised all 5 kids here, starting with J.D. at one month old, and graduated 2 kids from Southfield-Lathrup High School.

#2 – 2569 Towering Oaks Dr, White Lake, MI

This was two-story contemporary on 2.5 acres with 3 bedrooms, 2.5 baths, living room, dining room, kitchen with eat-in kitchenette, den and a "Mystery room." More about this room follows.

John and I were the "builders of record." We selected the lot, hired the architect and the trades. All went pretty smooth, except for some trouble with the brick layers and painters. They only seemed to listen if I stood there with the checkbook in my hand.

The brick layer was slow, but eventually got the job done with close supervision. The painter accidentally (?) lost control of his paint hose, paint spraying everywhere -- on me, my car, and the furnace company truck, but he did manage to miss John. Even after 27 "I'm sorry's, I didn't understand you's," etc., I fired him on the spot.

The biggest surprise: OUR MARRIAGE SURVIVED! Only 3 of the 7 family members actually moved into this home: John, JD and me.

Here's the story about the Mystery room. John and I were always there while the house was under construction, usually after the trades left for the day unless I particularly wanted to see something. One day, we were standing in the living room looking around. I looked up and asked, "What is that space for over the dining room?" We got out the blueprints and discovered it was dead space. So, being "the builder", …"excuse me, Mr. Plumber – can you move the toilet over here? and the sink there? And could you put a door there?" That dead space turned out to be the grandkid's favorite room in the house. From the Mystery Room you could see out over the dining room, living room, den, master bedroom, and eavesdrop on everything going on in the kitchen. The kids all took turns sleeping in the Mystery Room!

#3 – 6902 Ellinwood, White Lake, MI

We moved into Ellinwood from Lathrup Village. This was a 4,200 sq. ft. ranch with living room, dining room, first floor laundry, 7 bedrooms, a dark room, and a full, finished, walk-out to the Lake.

The entire family lived in this house. The two oldest had graduated high school, Cindi was just entering high school and would attend Lakewood High.

Two of our daughters married on the lakefront, Kim and Cindi. Both weddings were held outside with receptions at White Lake Oaks.

The weird dark room was rarely ever used and the door was kept closed most of the time. The only thing in the cupboards was a full set of dishes. The day we moved, the door was closed as usual, so the movers did not open it.

The dishes are probably still there.

Interesting: John came from a family of five (four boys and one girl) where the four boys slept in one bedroom with two sets of bunk beds. There was a single bathroom for all seven family members. I was an only child until the age of fourteen. I had my own bedroom. We sold this seven bedroom home to a couple with no children (??).

~ 7 ~

Why Get a 2nd Opinion (or 3, or 4, or even 5)?

In 1998 at the age of 63, I was enjoying a round of golf when suddenly I got a blind spot in my left eye. I finished the round, but after I got home I decided to make an appointment with a first class Ophthalmologist. John took me to the appointment and after an extensive exam I was told there was nothing wrong with either eye. "Just change reading glasses", I was told. But, then he also suggested I get a second opinion with a retina specialist.

The retina specialist examined me, and started me on steroids, but couldn't find anything either. So, he recommended a neurologist. To make a very, very long story short, I had many examinations by many different types of doctors, battery of tests and x-rays, but they all came up with nothing – clean bill of health all around. But I was rapidly losing weight and knew I was sick, but didn't know from what or where.

This goes on for quite some time. It's now March of 1999. I had a primary care doctor, who was also a customer of mine, and one Saturday I had to stop in his office to get some papers signed. When he came around the corner and saw me, he stopped short. "How much weight have you lost"? he asked. I told him I was down 50 pounds, ain't it great? He pointed to me and said "don't move, give me 20 minutes. John, don't let her move." He returned with 2 pieces of paper in his hand. He had scheduled me 3 appointments for the upcoming week. It occurred to me later that he definitely recognized something. Because he is who he is, that is why he was able to get appointments scheduled for me on a Saturday afternoon.

The first appointment was with a geriatric specialist; the second, an oncologist; the third for MRI's. The very next week I was checked into the hospital. Surrounded by John, my five kids and my mother, we were given the diagnosis – stage IV small cell lung cancer. It was a shock; I did not expect a death sentence of 3 to 6 months to live.

I couldn't imagine how I was going to handle all this. At one point, I looked around and saw 3 family members in the hospital room – my oldest, Deb, daughter-in-law, Betty and John. Deb was sitting with a notebook and pen writing notes and organizing things, I'm sure, Betty was leaning against the wall, arms folded, asking the most intelligent questions, and John had a clipboard and pen. I realized I had all the support I needed in my family and it appeared that each had taken on a specific role. That following Monday I began what would turn out to be a very long process, and was given my first dose of chemotherapy…the maximum amount, of course. Radiation treatments began at the same time.

This process took all spring and summer. I lost most of the year…my birthday, Easter, summer holidays. John was assisted by my kids who took turns coming out for a week at a time. Cindi and Deb, or JD and Kim, or some combination of siblings. Don and Betty were always there. I had visitors, which I don't really remember. I heard my office brought dinners to the house for months. Aunt Shirley visited and brought dinner every Friday. I was in and out of the hospital 3 or 4 times, sometimes taken by ambulance. I'm not aware of everything that went on during that period, and I'm told I don't really want to know. It was no small feat for the family to come home, Deb from California, Kim from Massachusetts, Cindi from Tennessee, Donald after work, JD from Georgia and my sister from California. Finally, I passed the critical stage.

Around September I began small feats. One week I worked on getting from my bedroom to the living room without the wheelchair. Maybe it was because by that time I had the house to myself and no one would know if I made it to the living room or not. Then I worked on getting into the kitchen to unload the dishwasher and put things away. Those little tasks helped bring me back into the living world.

My cancer had spread to my brain, causing a brain disease (PCD for short). At one time, we were told I would never walk or talk again, if I lived.

The miracle?   In addition to an outstanding team of doctors, aggressive treatment, God's mercy, and a supportive family, evidently, I have a unique antibody that fought off the brain disease.   The medical world has been studying my blood and my case.   I have been written up in the Journal of American Medicine and my case presented at neurological conferences nationwide.

It's been 18 years since my diagnosis, and my oncologist (the fabulous Dr. Owainati) only wants me to attend his Survivor Parties and to see me every other year.

~ 8 ~

I Can Draw A Straight Line Without a Ruler!

"My mom can't draw a straight line with a ruler!" was my daughter's comment to my art teacher when she found out I was taking art classes. I had signed up to take art class with a group of my friends, one who was teaching art on PBS.

When I was in grade school, I would look through my mother's magazines. There was always a little ad with a picture of an animal or something with a headline that said "Can you draw me?" I always drew the picture and sent it in. Although I never got a response, that didn't stop me.

In high school, I took anything "artsy". I loved tooling purses and belts, and chalk drawing. I actually signed up for an Art College, but changed my mind as I didn't think I could make a living at it.

During high school, I worked at a non-artsy job in downtown Detroit at Standard Accident Insurance Company. After graduation, I was promoted to an auditor. The next year I became engaged, a year after that I married, and then two years later I had my first child. I left Standard Accident and did not work again until my kids were all in school.

I never forgot about painting. I loved oil painting on canvas. It's the easiest and can readily be fixed. My favorites were landscapes. My least favorites were the "fruit in a bowl" or "vase of flowers." Another really good thing about oil...if you don't like it, cover it up and paint the next subject. I also loved ceramics.

This is my observation...I used to stand in the back of the classroom and observe everyone painting. I noticed if the person was painting a barn and that artist was short and fat, their barn would be short and fat. If the person was tall and skinny, their barn was tall and skinny. If the artist was just plain big...you know the rest.

I loved painting, but quit when I could no longer draw a straight line, even with a ruler.

(I am sorry, Gail, as you are the artist in our group, but this is my story.)

~ 9 ~
This Easter
I'll be a Methodist

My religion is Congregational according to my mother. I was baptized Congregational and as far back as we can see in her family, they were all Congregational. My dad's family did not practice a religion; I'm not sure he was even baptized.

We lived in Detroit from 1939 to 1947. The closest Protestant church was Baptist, so my parents sent me to Sunday school there. In 1947 when I was 12, we moved to Huntington Woods, Michigan. The closest Protestant church was Lutheran Missouri Synod. At age 12, Lutheran children go into Catechism. And are confirmed.

But I was not confirmed. The church Pastor, Pastor Winterstein lived across the street from us. One night we had a fire in the garage. A neighbor banged on the front door to wake us up. My dad called the fire department then quickly went out into the garage and pushed the car out of the garage. The reason it was so important to get the car out of the burning garage is that he had a case of whiskey in the back seat. After the fire was put out I remember my dad saying "that is why the fireman wear those big boots." Of the 12 bottles of whiskey, 3 were broken, 6 were missing and 3 were left intact.

Back to why I was not confirmed. Pastor Winterstein came to the house one day, and as always, my dad's Masonic bible was on the table. My dad was a 22nd Degree Mason and a Shriner. Evidently, being a Mason was against Missouri Synod Lutheran's rules. Pastor Winterstein said to me, "Marlene, you don't need to come to Catechism anymore," gesturing to the Bible. He said my dad was a sinner and I was not welcome in Catechism. I never told my mother or father what happened. I did not think my dad was a sinner even if he never went to church.

Then, in 1949 my parents moved to Lathrup Village and guess what kind of Protestant church was under construction? Community Congregational Church! I was of church age, so my mother and I went to church. My sister was baptized there, and when I was 20 years old I was married in the Congregational Church my mother and dad were married in.

My first husband Don and I lived in Berkley with two daughters both baptized in Community Congregational Church. In 1961, we moved to Sterling Heights where the closest church was a Lutheran Church of America. There, I finished Catechism and was confirmed, and my next two children were baptized there. They handled Don's funeral and was our church.

Then I met John, a Catholic. I called my Pastor and told him I was getting married. He was thrilled and made an appointment to meet John. The pastor told the story that in Germany, if there was a mixed marriage; the girls were raised Lutheran and the boys Catholic. He joked, "If my grandmother had been a grandfather, I would be a Priest instead of a Pastor." Anyway, John and I were married in the Catholic Church. At the altar stood both a Lutheran Minister and a Priest, and in the front pew sat my 4 kids. (Actually, that is not true…there were 3 kids. Dondi did not like his new suit and was in a bad mood, so Lynn Morgan was outside amusing him)

In 1969 we moved to White Lake. Our closest Protestant church was Christ of the Lakes with Pastor Sweitzer. Two more kids were confirmed and three married. Deb was married in a Lutheran church outside Las Vegas. JD has yet to marry. In 2000, Christ of the Lakes was sold.

When we recently moved to Milford, we discovered a non-denominational church, a Missouri Synod Lutheran, a Central Methodist, and a Presbyterian church.

I have probably selected a church for probably all the wrong reasons. Maybe because I have friends that go there; I love the choir; or the Pastor gives a good sermon. But it doesn't really matter as long as their foundation is in Christ, we're good.

This Easter, I'll be a Methodist.

~ 10 ~

What Do You Take For Granted?

I was talking on the phone to someone dear to me and far away in prison. She was telling me how much better she felt because some people from her church came visiting, bringing her news she was looking for.

Her boyfriend, who loves her and lives in the same apartment complex is paying her rent, car insurance and looks after things until she returns. But he had a heart attack and was in the hospital. In jail, her only communication with the outside world is a pay phone.

What do you take for granted?

Then she runs out of money for the pay phone and two weeks go by. Her sister puts some money on her account. So she calls the hospital and they tell her he is worse and could possibly die.

She calls me. I am very far away. She is worried that her rent, insurance and her car are going unpaid and it is the middle of the month. It is possible her furniture could be on the curb and her car towed away. What am I to do this far away? I make a few phone calls, leaving messages on answering machines. I have no answer for her.

Then the church people come back to visit. They found her boyfriend who was checked out of the hospital. He is weak, but alive. At the apartment they see her furniture, dusty, but there. Her car is in her regular parking place. If timing was different and all her furniture was tossed out to the curb and her car towed away, her license, birth certificate, title to the car would be gone.

What do you take for granted?

In prison you only get one outfit to wear. Deodorant, soap, shampoo, toothpaste are not provided for you. Snacks and sodas are luxury items. New tennis shoes are an extravagance.

What do you take for granted?

~ 11 ~

Every Generation Takes Care of Itself"

I am the record-keeper of my generation for my mother. My mother was born, raised, married, and lived in Michigan until she turned 92.

She then sold virtually everything, including her house. I selected some things, as did her family in California, some of my kids and her friends. The items she kept were loaded onto a moving van, and she and my sister Cristie boarded an airplane headed west. She moved in with my sister, got a California driver's license, bought a car and resumed her life.

She came home only one time, so I threw a party and all the Michigan relatives came. We went to her church, and had a good time.

Between the age of 93 and 99, in her family babies born, relatives died, and Michigan folks carried on with their lives. In California, babies were born and people died, and the Californian's carried on with their lives. Except for me keeping tabs, family in one state really didn't know what family in the other state was doing or even what they looked like today.

So, for my mother's Christmas gift the year she turned 99, I sent out e-mails, notes, Facebook posts, and early Christmas cards asking family and friends to send me their family portrait. I urged them to go to K-Mart, JC Penney, or a Walmart photographer, or even to their neighbor, just please send me a photograph. "The Book" was born.

I assembled her family tree and her life with photos. I had a picture of my mother at 6 months, in school, her graduation picture, wedding, 50th anniversary. I collected our wedding photos, graduation, 3 different 5 generation photos. I had all 8 grandchildren and their kids, plus five great, great, grandchildren.

Christmas morning she opened "The Book." She scanned a few pages, picked it up and took it into her bedroom to go through it in private. Connecting with memories. She then brought it back out to show everyone and discuss who was who in each photo.

Since that Christmas, "The Book" has been shared at get-togethers, parties, and funerals – including my mother's own funeral. She died just short of her 100th birthday.

The moral of this story is that someone in each family should be the keeper of those memories and to keep track of who is who in the family. Keeping photos on a cell phone is convenient, but they are not easily shared, or is one able to carry something like "The Book" into one's bedroom to be transported back in time, generation by generation.

~ 12 ~

Can You Read *Cursive*?

Cursive is a writing style in which the strokes are joined together in each word.

On April 18, 2016, I heard a small blurb on TV about teaching kids "cursive" handwriting. The teacher said we don't have time to teach it in class, the kids are only taught to sign their name as they would on a check or legal document. Hummm...I wondered if they can't write it, could they read cursive?

I personally have enjoyed all my friends' handwriting on Christmas, birthday and get well cards. And in each, the handwriting is very different and distinct. Some even mix cursive and printing.

I remember when I was sick, my handwriting was unreadable. Today, when I get something written from a friend and it doesn't look like their handwriting should, I wonder if something is wrong.

Of all my family and friends, my dad's handwriting was the most beautiful. My grandmother wrote very small and backhanded. My cousin also wrote small with meticulous letters. I'm sure you can recognize famous signatures like Abraham Lincoln and John Hancock.

I've noticed many companies still use cursive...look at J.L. Hudson, Henry Ford and Ford products, Hallmark and Cadillac. The City of Milford uses cursive. How many do you notice?

I hope the younger generation learns to write cursive, can read it, and appreciates the beauty of a handwritten note.

~ 13 ~
Dating

For many years, I lived in a neighborhood where everyone
was married and raising kids. My friend and neighbor,
Nancy, was the first to become single after her husband
left her for another woman. I became the second, a
widow, after Don died in a car accident. My friend Nancy
had to work, I did not, and I stayed home and was a full-
time mom.

One day, Nancy was invited to a party. The host had recently been
transferred to Michigan, was a bachelor, and threw the party to meet people.
The invitation said to bring and friend and a hors d'oeuvre. She brought me
as the friend; I don't remember what the hors d'oeuvre was.

The bachelor/host was John Dooling. We began dating and went out to
dinner a few times. He came to the house for dinner a few times and got to
meet the kids. John took the whole family to the zoo, Ice Capades, and the
State Fair. Sometimes we would go down to my dad's boat which was
docked on the Detroit River near Sinbad's restaurant.

My friends wanted to meet this guy. They got together and hosted a "Meet John Night" at a local restaurant. John's friends, who were all bachelors, wanted to meet me as well. One friend had a boat on Lake St. Clair named "Happy Hour." Nancy and I would hire babysitters once or twice a month and spend time on the boat with John and his friends.

John's family also wanted to meet me. My mom and dad agreed to babysit, and John and I flew to Philadelphia to meet the Dooling clan. John had 4 brothers and 1 sister (his mom and youngest brother were dead). So here I am to meet John's dad, all his siblings along with their spouses and children. John had never been married. I do not know what his family thought of this widow with 4 children ages 9, 7, 4 and 1; I can only imagine the conversation after we left!

On April 7, 1967 John proposed. My response was a conditional "if you, me, and the kids are still interested in 6 months, then my answer is YES."

I guess we were all still interested, because we were married on September 22, 1967. My sister was my Matron of Honor and John's brother Jim was his Best Man. We were married in the Catholic Church with both the Priest and my Lutheran Minister at the Alter. Friends, and families from Philadelphia and Michigan attended and a great time was had by all.

September 22, 2016 will mark our 49th anniversary!

~ 14 ~

100 Years of Alcatraz

The infamous Alcatraz was still a prison when John and I got a special tour of the island in 1970 on our way back from Hawaii. There were no prisoners there because it had been officially shut down as a prison in 1963. The buildings were empty, dilapidated, and full of trash and debris. The previous year, an activist group of Native Americans took over the island and claimed the land for "all Indian tribes." They had been ousted just prior to our tour.

We saw the cells of famous prisoners like Al "Scarface" Capone, Robert Stroud the "Birdman of Alcatraz", "Machine Gun" Kelly, and Arthur Barker who was public enemy #1 and the creepy one of Ma Barker's gang. The tour was dark and it felt odd being there. Jail is a strange place to me.

One part of the tour I will never forget was when I went into a solitary confinement cell. That was terrifying. It was so dark and stone quiet. I could actually hear my own heart beating in my chest. I can see why it was an effective punishment.

The prison on Alcatraz Island claimed that no one could escape. Situated on this small island about a mile and a half off the coast of San Francisco, the tides were so strong and the waters so cold that anyone would drown quickly. In fact, there were 14 attempted escapes involving 36 prisoners. It is reported that 23 were recaptured, 6 shot and killed, 2 drown, and the remaining 5 missing and presumed drowned.

In 1861, Alcatraz was used as a civil war prison; in 1868 it became a military prison, and in 1934 began operating as a Federal prison. Since 1972 the island became part of the Golden Gate Recreation Area and opened to the public in 1973. In 1986 it became a historic landmark.

~ 15 ~

The Grand Matriarch
& the Grand Mutt!

Frances M. Emblin   Fred W. Emblin

Born: December 10, 1914   Born: May 20, 1913

Died: October 17, 2014   Died: April 11, 1985

This article is a lot about my Mother and some about my Dad.

My Mother was also known as Papa or Fran. She jokingly liked to remind us not to forget she was the oldest woman in the family, and as the Grand Matriarch, she was to be treated with respect. Always followed by that smile of hers.

My Dad, Fred, called all of my kids either "mutt" or "pill." Even after all these years, the kids still refer to my dad as "Grandpa Mutt." Funny how nicknames just stick around forever.

My mother resided in Lathrup Village from 1949 through 2008 in the house my dad built in 1949.

Frances came from a family that fought in The Revolutionary War. She retired after almost 40 years as a nursery school teacher, and was an Eastern Star. She loved to play bridge and attend bible study. Fred was the building superintendent for the Shrine of the Little Flower in Detroit. He was a 22nd Degree Mason and a Shriner.

Frances was preceded in death by her parents Myrtle & Arthur Mills, her husband Fred, her son-in-Law Don Rhoten, Sisters Gladys and Ion, Great-Grandson Dean and Brother Roger. Fred was preceded in death by parents Maude and Al Emblin, Brother Vaughn & 2 sisters, Shirley Rowbotham & Elaine Chivas.

Frances & Fred have eight grandchildren, Deborah (Don) Danko, Kimberly Dangleis, Cindi (Jeff) Curry, Donald (Betty) Rhoten, John J. Dooling Jr., Michelle (Cory) Oogjen, Nichole (Ed) Dzuiba, and Brett (Jennifer) Morse.

Great-Grandchildren are Billy (Brittany) Dangleis, Kelly Moriarty, Dean Dangleis (deceased), Nicholas (Linda) Curry, Ian Curry, Samantha Rhoten, Makayla and Madison Oogjen, Brooklyn Baldock, Olivia, Abigail and Jackson Dzuiba, and Sierra and June Morse.

Great-Great Grandchildren: Kaylee & Kadence Moriarity, Bailey and Bradley Dangleis, and Colin and Sloan Curry.

Her family loved her deeply and she will be missed by all.

My mother and I were best friends. For decades, we went shopping almost every Saturday, and we either spoke or saw each other several times a week, and were bridge partners. I miss her a lot and dedicate my portion of this book to her.

I am now the oldest woman in my family, but I will never be able to fill the shoes of my mother, The Grand Matriarch.

~ Five Generation Photos ~

144

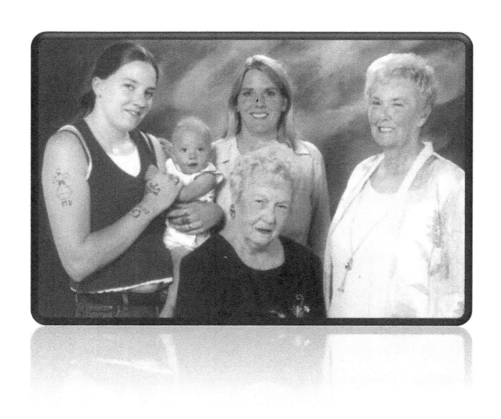

Max Kirschke

ARCHIVES

&

ADVENTURES

. . . the hodgepodge of life

To my parents Willy Emil and Helene Johanna Kirschke who brought me into this world, raised me, nurtured me to adulthood, and demanded, I dedicate this initial contribution of memories

ACKNOWLEDGEMENTS

I have brought writings of my experiences to those named below. They have had everything to do with publication of my stories. They have encouraged, refined, and helped prepare them to share. They have had much to do with the outcome you will read. The experiences are mine to be sure but their comments, criticisms, and corrections were invaluable.

Susan McCoy who since March 2014 has inspired me and guided me in the production of words and provided revelations in my presentations that brought about regular rewrites to the stories. Her inspirational suggestions brought me to share memories and experiences with those I love who previously were unaware of events and struggles in my life.

Rose, the most important person in my life who has encouraged me throughout our relationship in everything I have attempted and who was the first to hear what I had written and provided comment thereon.

Lisa Giese, a beloved stepdaughter who was the first to accept with enthusiasm the challenge of bringing this to publication readiness despite unimaginable responsibilities as wife, mother of four, and executive at a major corporation.

Carol Bagdady, a daughter in law, a reader of the printed word beyond the meaning of avid, mother of three, an attorney, the achievement of later life desire, now employing her skills, experience, education. and knowledge in a position of prominence at a major labor organization, who found time for me in this first endeavor at writing.

Eric Kirschke, my youngest son, employed at a major automotive company utilizing his abilities in automotive design, engineering, and computer knowledge, who on many evenings assisted in preparing my contribution to this anthology into the form demanded by the publisher.

To the people in my life, the co-authors of this anthology, the members of my extended family all of who make my life so rich and enjoyable.

WHO AM I?

A speck of dust on a grain of sand born Winfred Max Kirschke, known commonly as "Max", on February 13, 1932 to parents of German birth, citizens of the USA, the country they loved. Brother to Bill, retired in Traverse City, MI.

Born, raised, educated, married, and worked my entire life in the city I love, Detroit.

Detroit Free Press/Flagstar Marathon

Now married to Rose, the love of my life, for over seventeen years.
Senior member of a blended family that numbers nine children, twenty eight grandchildren, and now six great grandchildren that provide unending joy.

Also an individual, continuously evolving, who has lived, loved, and is loved by people held dear. A person who has dislikes, opinions, and tales of experiences to share.
A retiree, enjoying each moment gardening, volunteering, and pursuing interests. A man with the hope that what is revealed herein, will ignite the image the reader possesses and instill the desire to record and share.

Paper and pen is all you need.

FOREWORD

One may not have a plan or even a goal as a young person. I believe few do. However, that does not mean that one should not be aware that there are paths to choose, values to discover, and memories to record in the process of reaching adulthood and as we age. We have all experienced joys and sorrow, success and disappointment, beauty and perhaps horror.

We are the curators of our shimmering images. Is it not our duty to preserve our images for those who we care about and for those who care about us?

CONTENTS

I

Recalling Childhood Memories

(161-174)

PA'S BAKERY ROUTE

It is with much contemplation that I begin with the events that I can recall from my early life. Not too long ago I believed the days of my early life were too far distant to recall. An over eighty year old photograph album compiled by my father brought forth forgotten visions, hidden surprises, and strong memories that jump started my brain cells. Discovering other long forgotten pictures and memorabilia added their essence to the recovery process.

I am troubled with the definition of love for my parents. What does a three or four year old or even a twelve year old know about love? In those childhood days that word was not a part of the vocabulary. It was acceptance of what was. I knew respect, obedience, joy, and perhaps childish anger whenever denied. Only in my adult years could I translate my parents' words and actions into love. The rigors of growing into manhood were in the way then.

My earliest memory is being Pa's helper on a bakery route to Ann Arbor, a considerable distance from Detroit in those days. Stoyke's German American Bakery was a well-known name among the German immigrant community and my father drove a truck vending the baked goods door to door. Occasionally he would take me with him to this college town. As we traveled, the delicious aroma of fresh baked bread from the back of the van became overwhelming and I hoped there would be something for me at the end of the day. He would drop me off at the Feldhauser's to play with their two daughters and eventually return so we could make our way back home. I heard the "aah-ooga" of the horn when he arrived.

163

Pa opened the rear doors of the truck and I remember clambering unto the rear bumper and reaching in to find a treat. I was four then and I still love fresh baked Danish pastry, especially cherry.

WAR!

I was seven. Brother Bill was five. On one September Sunday afternoon in 1939 we were on our way to the home of Onkel Hans and Tante Erna, Pa's sister, when we passed a street corner where a newsboy was heralding war. This extra edition of the newspaper blurted the unwelcome news that Germany had invaded Poland.

Bill and I knew that war had been a part of Pa's life. He was eighteen in 1914 when he volunteered and served in the German army. On that fateful September day the headline meant little and it was only in the late forties that I realized the magnitude of that event insofar as it affected our father.

Although he immigrated in 1928 and became an American citizen, on July 1, 1935, his German origin made him suspect for anti-American activities. More than once FBI agents came to our home and interviewed Pa. These strangers may have caused some apprehension for us but Pa's assurances that everything was okay calmed our childish fears. He was, for a significant time, not allowed to work in a factory that provided war materials for our country. When he was finally allowed, he produced more than was required despite union personnel admonitions.

He never allowed whatever misfortune that came to him to filter down to his sons. We were very fortunate boys. I have often wondered how he managed, but he did and without rancor.

His tolerance for issues that confronted him aided Bill and I in our growth and attitude toward the unpleasant circumstances we would later face.

The older we became the greater the appreciation for the lessons learned in childhood.

HOT DOGS AND ICE CREAM

MEMORIES OF LONG LAKE

Nearly every Sunday morning during the summer my brother Bill and I would jump into the back seat of old Henry, the family Ford that once more would deliver us to Long Lake for another day of joy. Pa was the president of the Berliner Verien, a club for German speaking immigrants. Each Sunday the members would gather and the smoky spicy aroma of bratwurst would permeate the air and the porter and stout flowed. We youngsters quickly found our way to the water.

About 1940 the club necessarily disbanded. Apparently any German organization or officer thereof was under suspicion of conducting activities that would benefit the Nazi regime under Adolph Hitler. However, four couples decided to continue the weekly Sunday summer tradition and purchased the property next to the one the club rented. It is here that my memories reside.

The men constructed the sturdy picnic tables placing them in the shade of the huge oak tree that dominated the property. The tables waited for the ladies to arrive on Sunday morning. Ma cleared our table of twigs and leaves before placing the red checkered picnic oil cloth on it. Later Pa would pump up the fuel cylinder of the well-used Coleman camp stove so that the potato pancakes and warm applesauce could be prepared.

I remember sizzling bacon served crisp on a BLT, hot soup and brats with German potato salad being our fare in those days. Brother Bill and I, of course, were in the water before old Henry's engine had cooled but we never had to be called twice for lunch.

The trip to the lake seemingly took forever. What was then farm country and spacious fields became Northland, our first regional shopping center, and the skyscrapers of Southfield. Often the Schleys', with son Jerry and the Bundes' the oldest couple of the four, were already there making preparations for guests of the families that had purchased the property. Strangely, Pa's sister Erna and husband and their twin sons rarely came out to the lake although they were partners.

When the guests arrived, it wasn't long before the horseshoe stakes were planted and play began. We looked forward to Sunday each week and occasionally we were allowed to invite a neighborhood pal to accompany us.   Other youngsters arrived with their parents and we all enjoyed the splashing and venturing into deep water before heeding the long awaited call for lunch. I remember we all had to wait for an hour before going back into the water. The narrative was that we would suffer cramps and perish if we did not obey.

Two isolated but wonderful memories of this time come to mind. On our way home, Pa occasionally would stop at a roadside foot long hot dog stand on Northwestern Highway and Bill and I would be treated to one. Also, on rare occasion, we would go West on Commerce road, beyond Long's Apple Orchard to Cape's ice cream parlor in Milford. Imagine a two scoop cone of your favorite or even exotic choice. That was living!

Long Lake remained important in our lives through high school and for years thereafter. Bill and *I* were very lucky boys a fact we discovered only years later. The great depression was ending and World War II was well under way.

In our high school teen years, Jerry, Bill, and I hosted outings at Long Lake for our groups. Jerry and I had developed a close relationship and were members of the same high school social group. Bill had selected Wilbur Wright as his high school of choice.

In our twenties and both married, Jerry and I continued the Sunday tradition. The tradition was immensely enhanced when Jerry uncorked his superior bottles of wine, superior to mine at least. Those were the days!!!

My three sons as well enjoyed the lake property until it was sold. Three generations had benefited from Pa's decision to buy.

Property: long gone. Memories: Alive and vibrant!

GRADE SCHOOL EXPERIENCES
ELEMENTARY

Hutchinson elementary was plunked into the center of the residential community unlike the schools of today which are on expansive campuses. It was a rectangular two story brick building between French Road and Montclair Avenue just one half block north of Warren Avenue.

We lived one block over at 5053 Harding Avenue. To get to school we cut through DeDona's yard that had a massive tart cherry tree in the backyard that Mrs. DeDona allowed us to climb and harvest each summer. We ran up the alley to Pitzer's yard on French Road where the safety patrol boys would allow us to cross to the gravel school yard. I remember more about the yard where we played baseball nearly every day during the summer than I do about my learning in the classrooms.

I know that E, S, and U were the grades we carried home on report cards that required a parental signature when returned. We were graded on scholarship and citizenship and we needed a passing grade for mom and dad. Teacher's remarks that kept parents aware of progress were important side bars. There were consequences for failure but we never discovered of what they consisted. What elementary aged boy would want to find out? Most certainly not me!

The north end of Hutchinson's first floor had a music room, an arts room, a library, and a wood shop. The auditorium, gym, and science room with its conservatory facing French Road were at the south end of the building. So was the office of Henrietta VanDyke, our principal. The second floor was where we learned our A, B, C's and that two plus two were four.

I have two very strong grade school memories. My seventh grade English teacher, Mrs. Kingsbury insisted that I should practice my handwriting with my right hand and made me place my paper in a position on my desk like the rest of the class did. To make my letters slant properly my left hand would rub over the letters written on previous lines and often I would have a smudged page. Mrs. Kingsbury stood over me occasionally and got my attention by rapping my knuckles with her ruler to emphasize whatever point she was trying to make. Her words were discouraging and I heard how quiet the room became. More than once there was a general twitter or snickering but it wasn't funny to this lefthander.

Mr. Plia taught math. It was in his eighth grade class that he became the source of my most unpleasant remembrance. He would not differentiate my name Winfred, from Winifred Sherman, so quite often he would berate me fiercely for failing to respond when called upon. A combination of anger and humiliation always came over me as I stood to reply to a question. I could not muster the courage to correct him.

Although my thoughts at the time were not about Winifred, I now wonder how she endured this unending situation. He never got it right nor did he ever apologize. I managed to survive the embarrassment until graduation.

Graduation provides me with my most pleasant and lasting memory. We sat in the auditorium to listen to our principal address us. Mrs. VanDyke's final words to us were" Know Thyself". I have been working on that for a lifetime.

II

Valuable Lessons

(175-190)

TEEN JOBS

VALUE 'TEEN' JOB OPPORTUNITIES

Upon reflection, it seems I have been working for a lifetime. My teen years were great rewarding years. And importantly it was time for a boy to evolve into a young man and lay a foundation for manhood.

At age twelve I was carrying the afternoon edition of "The Detroit Times" newspaper from station A4 on Fairview and Canfield just a short walk from Southeastern High School. My route was Harding from Canfield to Warren. Although our home was on Harding just six houses North of Warren, my route was blatantly a different neighborhood.

This inconsequential job may have been the most important one in my formation. I was a little business man needing to collect from the seventy or so customers and paying for the papers on Saturday afternoon. It wasn't always easy. Accounts payable was not an acceptable option. My neighborhood was segregated, a word I was to discover the meaning of much later in life. Segregation was not a concept known to me. Yes, I noticed the primarily Caucasian population lived North of Warren and the Black South of Warren. I never contemplated why.

David Smith was the only black student in grade school and his parents lived on my route. I will admit that greeting so many black faces on Friday collection night the first few times was a bit scary. It wasn't long before their skin color faded and revealed faces, feelings, attitudes that were the same as the multi ethnic street where I lived.

The appearance of the neighborhood was no different from mine. Homes and properties were well cared for and exhibited a pride similar to that which my dad had. All became more than my customers. I didn't know it then, but for this young boy, they were teachers. I learned from them the equality of the human condition, at least as it should be.

One Saturday I was delivering and collecting when suddenly I developed a continuous nose bleed. One of my customers called me into her home, sat me down, and began laying her hands upon me. Shortly, the bleeding ended and I was able to continue on my route without incident. I learned later that she had a reputation as a healer. I cannot recall having a nose bleed since.

At several of the homes, there were two stacks of coins on a table. One stack was for the paper boy. The other was for the "numbers man" that also collected on Saturdays. Each of us knew to which stack we belonged. These years and experiences were perhaps the most important formative years in my life.

I cannot remember how I fell into my next work experience but there I was, an employee at The Great Atlantic and Pacific Tea Co. I stocked shelves at night and was a bagger, a skill that had to be learned. Baggers in those days also carried the bags to the parking lot for the customer.

Soon I became a worker in the fresh meat department. Packaging, weighing and pricing were my tasks until Stan, my boss, showed me how to display packages in the counter. He even put me in charge of maintaining the smoked and processed meat counter. On Saturday morning I had to be there before 5:00am to assist with the unloading of sides and quarters of beef that weighed more than I did. Thankfully the drivers helped and taught me how to carry the load without it winding up on the sawdust covered floor of the meat cutting room.

Our store at Gratiot and Rohns had two fulltime butchers. Today, the big store meat department does very little, if any, butchering. One more advancement for me was to the position of fish and chicken preparer. Fifty whole and processed chickens were in each iced down crate that I dragged out of the cooler. Stan taught me how to disassemble a chicken into its various saleable components and how to package them including the innards that came in a bag with each chicken. Fish had to be scaled, beheaded and filleted, one more learning experience and skill to be developed.

We were not open on Sundays at that time so there were items in the counter that could not be held over the weekend. It included beef that had begun to darken and fish to some extent. Small amounts were allowed to be taken home. Stan knew from experience how much meat to cut and package and fish to process for the counter and there was not too much to choose from on Saturday night.

It remains a bonanza in my mind. Our family ate quite well in those days. My mom enjoyed fish, dad did not. Fairly often my mom and I would sit down for a fish dinner together. At this young age I grew to appreciate food at all levels, it's preparation at the stores, the packaging and display, the huge variety available, the preparation at home, and of course it's consumption. Today, I still look forward to things I have not experienced from a culinary standpoint, and although I have favorites, I will not exclude.

My final teen work experience came at Dodge Main, A Chrysler Corporation facility. The father of my best friend Dick Shields' had an important position at the factory. As a result, Dick and I both were hired as line employees at this facility. The second year at Wayne State University was coming soon. At the time, the superior pay offered by the automotive companies allowed us to accumulate the necessary cash to pay the costs of education and provide enough walking around money so that working during the school year was unnecessary.

The work I had to do was the most mind numbing I could imagine. As the line unendingly moved by my station carrying the rear axle housing, I, file in hand, was required to remove a metal burr from one area of the housing. It was robotic work accomplished by human hands. Thankfully I became a machine tender not long after. The machine countersunk the fastener holes in the very same housing on the very same line that moved at the very same maddening pace.

I used to pray for a breakdown which came often enough when a tool broke on my machine. I would then remove each housing from the line and place it on the floor. My station was never down too long. Then came the contest of putting the product from the floor unto the machine and then unto the line, filling each empty carrier as the line moved. Breakdowns were my savior in maintaining my sanity.

Summers end and the beginning of the school year could not have come at a better time. I was ready to conclude this chapter of my working life. However, I had learned that knowing an influential person in a position of power that could assist you was a valuable asset, and most importantly, working on an automotive line despite the excellent pay was not for me.

THE SEED OF SELF EMPLOYMENT

My father in law was Gustave Einar Headbloom. Korsoft Engineering was one of Gus senior's rare failures. That failure, however, offered me the first opportunity for an entrepreneurial experience.

George Sobosky was a big Hungarian teddy bear kind of man who was a welder with considerable skills in tool and die repair. He occupied the Korsoft facility a building somewhat larger than a two car garage on Mt. Elliott and was employing the assets owned by the defunct Korsoft broach manufacturing enterprise.

In the spring of 1956 brother-in-law, Gust Jr. asked me if I would be interested in assisting George operate his welding business. It was a Saturday job of billing and bookkeeping which included paying the bills, one of which was a $100 check to Gus Senior for the rental of the building and all the equipment which included arc welders, a Heli arc, heaters and furnaces, and various smaller equipment and tools. Even in the mid 1950's that was a pittance and one hell of a deal for George. Father and son were doing everything in their power to assist with his success.

To expand services we purchased a revolutionary metalizing machine that would spray steel particles onto a worn shaft to bring it back to a diameter so that after machining the device could once again perform its intended function.

Fitzsimons Manufacturing, a tool and die customer just up the street on the corner of East Outer Drive, asked George if he had any interest in securing production work. We talked about what it could mean for company growth, income for George, and profit. The workload for a tool and die welder depended on when a customer would call, usually in an emergency situation. Many days could possibly pass without a call and there would be others where the workload was enormous.

We decided to try. We established a rate per hour that would provide our goals. George would tell me how long he would estimate it would take to join components into the desired assembly, a skill I would soon learn to master without assistance from George. We were fortunate and soon George was unable to complete all the work that was required to properly serve the customer.

Our first hire was a young Ralph Ciccotelli who acquired the skills that were taught with enthusiasm. Ralph thoroughly enjoyed his job. His work ethic was phenomenal, and later his people skills would surface. It wasn't long before the incoming work became overwhelming and more decisions had to be made. As the spokesperson for George, I recommended to his board of directors the purchase of a somewhat larger building that had become available a few hundred feet south of the facility we rented. The purchase was approved and after venting equipment was installed, George and Ralph moved in and began hiring as production work began to outpace tool and die repair by multiples. I hired a young lady who lived in one of the few residences facing Mt. Elliott and she performed the work that I had been doing. I remained as a part time weekend overseer of the operation.

Also in the mid 1950's Metallic Inert Gas Shielded welding technology, or wire welding, was just becoming available and more common and at an affordable price. At an American Welding Society show George, Ralph, and I saw our first MIG welding machine. Before this the production arc welding of assemblies was accomplished with a mineral covered welding electrode perhaps twelve inches in length. Wire welding consisted of a sixty pound coil on a reel, the electrode, shielded by carbon dioxide gas instead of the mineral covering. Our production assemblies were joined by the brazing method and we felt expansion into arc welding would be beneficial.

We purchased the welder. I am confident that George Welding Co. was among the first "job shops" with this highly efficient method. It became and remains the method of choice in the production welding of automotive assemblies. We continued our growth with the board of directors consistently approving the steps we were taking.

The die was cast for my future but realization would remain years away. A regular job, meaning full time employment for me, began in 1954 before graduation from Wayne State University. It included several years at Ford Motor Company and shorter times at Apex Broach and Machine Co. and Security Aluminum Company. I enjoyed my work at each firm, but I knew what would make me happiest in my working life. The possibility of self-employment was most important and strangely it had little to do with income expectations. It had everything to do with outcomes from decisions made.

The opportunity arose in 1961. The part time work experience was about to blossom into the reality I was hoping to achieve.

S&O WELDCRAFT

In early 1961 I read in the classifieds of the Detroit News an advertisement that offered the sale of a welding business. It was as if I had been struck by a bolt of lightning. Somehow I knew that this could become my opportunity to achieve the goal I sought.

I had been working for George Welding Company on a part time basis since the mid 1950's. It had become a successful small business. Diversification, enthusiastic workers, high quality service, and vision for the future contributed to its success.

Once again I submitted a plan to expand to the board of directors, this time through acquisition. The board listened and agreed that we should move forward. They decided as well that a new corporation would be formed and that whatever the needed capital requirements were, including operating funds, it would be provided by the existing enterprise George Welding Company. Ralph Ciccotelli and I would be offered equal shares in the new venture.

S&O Weldcraft was located on Michigan Avenue at 23rd street on the West side of Detroit. It was a company with a reputation of high quality tool and die welding. The purchase was made and the name retained. I became the operating head of this facility.

At our rear door was the huge Star Tool & Die Co., our largest customer. The former owner of S&O, Mr. Oullette, introduced me to his larger customers in the first two weeks as I learned the ropes of his business. The transition went well. It was my intent to make production welding assemblies the primary volume producing segment of this business without affecting the tool and die repair portion of the business as had been accomplished for George Welding Company.

During subsequent visits to my customers, and at times when I was making pickups of tool and die work, I indicated that we were looking for production assembly work. We were modestly successful in securing short run assembly work. One customer, Whitehead Stamping had successfully bid on a Automotive Tank Command assembly that required welding. They were unequipped for welding and S&O bid and won the contract to provide the welding.

We began delivering the product and during this time an ethical problem arose that I did not feel I could resolve without advice. The production manager at Whitehead approached me and asked if I would consider paying a "commission" if he could enhance the price we were receiving for the assembly we were producing. The request took me by surprise.

I was aware of the practice of lunch dates and gift giving from sales representatives to purchasing agents but this appeared highly improper. Bob White of McClain and White, our accountants and my mentor Gust Jr. both advised refusal of the request.

My response to the proposal was that I could not in good conscience accept the arrangement.

Although loss of the work was a possibility, we kept the job without price increase until the contract was fulfilled. The importance of the decision and its fallout did not become evident until years later, when the company's owner and president called me and asked if I had ever been approached to pay an amount to one of his employees in return for an increase in billing. It isn't often when a decision made years earlier is brought into focus as clearly as this one was.

At the time the decision was being made to ignore the offer, Gust Jr. revealed a policy of his company. Lunch with a supplier was acceptable only if the employee paid the tab, which would then be reimbursed by the company, but under no circumstances could a gift or even a lunch be accepted.

Another of the existing accounts was Detroit Engineering & Machine Co., owned by the Kellman brothers. It was the largest metal stamping company outside the "big three" automotive facilities.

Barney Crosley was the plant manager and John Olinek headed the engineering department. A thirty to forty man welding department was contained in the huge facility. On one occasion while I was picking up a die to be repair welded, I had the opportunity to speak with both and indicated that I would like to secure production welding work as well.

The company was ready to begin producing the 1963 model Corvette front bumper assembly and apparently lacked the room to initiate the production. I jumped at the opportunity that Barney and John offered.

This assembly became the "hallmark", the single most important assembly of my business life.

Upon introduction, the sales of the newly styled Corvette skyrocketed. The welding assembly fixture provided by Demco could not produce enough assemblies to meet the demand. The plan volume had been set too low and it was too late to build additional tools. In addition quality problems arose.

My people and I undertook the task of determining how to increase production which we accomplished by separating the workload called for by the welding/locating fixture. Quality problems were addressed and resolved as well.

It wasn't long after the successful launch that additional production work was offered which we gladly accepted. Mr. Crosley asked if I was ready to accept metal stamping work on presses he would provide. My lack of knowledge or experience in metal forming prompted me to decline this offer. Business life was becoming hugely exciting!

S&O Weldcraft had achieved its goal in less than two years. We could not take on another assembly. The five thousand square foot building floor space was totally consumed with work nearly all from DEMCO. The situation became intolerable. Further expansion was imperative.

III

Search for Wisdom

And Understanding

(191-214)

A JOURNEY OF FAITH

All of 84 years on this planet have passed for me and religion remains the mystery it has always been. It's birth and development in me has been at best accidental in much more than one half of my life. Truthfully none of the incidents described below were a part of a conscious journey before I believed. Belief arrived in an instant at a life altering event.

To begin, my parents had me baptized shortly after birth at Holy Trinity Lutheran Church in downtown Detroit. I believe it was the home church of the German immigrant population in the early 1930s. My next encounter with the religious community arrived when I was thirteen.

I literally was dragged off the street by an evangelical pastor in front of Luther Memorial Evangelical Church on Warren Avenue and Garland just three short blocks from home. I faithfully attended the instruction classes and became a member of the church. Soon after acceptance secular interests including sports, education, friendships, and freedom lured me away.

Upon reflection, it would be fair to say that my mom and dad possessed a belief of sorts although neither attended worship services. They provided me with my first Bible, the King James Version, which has become a treasure of mine. It has resided quietly in my bookcase for some seventy years. The aged and tattered cover belie the nearly pristine condition of its pages. Perhaps expectantly it waits for me to rediscover the poetic like versus and seventeenth century words as thy, thine, and thou and ye among others.

Modern Americanized versions, much preferred for ease of reading and understanding, in some way, for me at least, detract from the beauty of the language.

During the first fifty years or so of my life, marriage, baptisms, funerals, and somewhat regular attendance at Easter and Christmas services were the extent of my participation in religious activities. Worship was not dormant. It did not exist! If there was a level of belief, it would have been impossible to define.

All three of our sons were baptized at Immanuel Lutheran on Chandler Park Drive in Detroit by pastor Reverend Constantine Trued who also married my first wife, Bert and I years earlier. That was the last time the three sons saw the inside of a church until their marriage or at least until they had moved out of the house.

In my early adult years when experience and decisions were beginning to develop my character, I was clueless with regard to the factors that entered into that formation.

Since then I have come to believe that there is a moral code implanted in each of us. Perhaps part of our DNA. It is reinforced and developed as a result of parenting, the observation of others' behavior, the process of aging, and the experiences that one encounters. This nurtured code manifests itself as conscience, that barely audible voice, that feeling, that rises in oneself when "wrong" is being considered as a path when "good" and "evil" are the choices.

One can and some say that the tiny voice is the Holy Spirit who religion tells us is our guide. Whatever actions I was taking throughout my early adult life had no religious connotation, at least so I thought at the time. It was not until much later that this barely audible voice that gives me a sense of awe about nature, right and wrong, and the gift and ability to choose, was connected with religion. Perhaps the commandments taught and learned at thirteen provided the background for decisions in my life. At the time, there was no connection.

In the mid 1980's, the realization of the existence of a supreme being was forever indelibly confirmed in an instant. I exclaimed "Oh God", as the .38 caliber projectile entered my chest.

Five explosions later, seriously wounded, near death I was told later, the emergency vehicle with its paramedics sped me to Detroit's Receiving Hospital just a few minutes from the scene. The hospital chaplain offered a prayer for me as I was wheeled into the areas where the team of professionals proceeded to save my life...miraculously so!

I believed! The journey of faith had begun. All that had gone before as described to this point were unconnected incidents of life not at all considered a part of a faith journey. How differently I view everything now!

After recovery, little developed in my now journey. Perhaps forty or so years of ignoring worship played a role. Prayer, of sorts became a part of my being. Churched believers would likely scoff at the idea that what I was doing was praying.

Often I thought that, but I continued. I became absorbed with the question of why had I been spared? What was to be my ordained mission? Would it ever be revealed? Was there truly a mission?

It wasn't until early 1998, after the death of my wife, Bert, that I finally sought comfort in a church community. Having been baptized and instructed in the Lutheran tradition, I gravitated to Christ Lutheran in Milford whose pastor Richard Pape and the 200 family congregation welcomed me as a member of their family with enthusiasm that pleasantly surprised me.

I became very active and volunteered as a laborer among many that were rehabbing the original small white wooden structure on the East side of the property that had served as the original church. The building was being used for Sunday school activities and was the home of a local AA group. The rehab project was to prepare the building for a pre-school and Kindergarten program that the congregation had decided to offer. My enthusiastic volunteer activities prompted the congregation leaders to award me the job of treasurer. I had found a comfort zone in my journey and all aspects of my life were headed in a positive direction.

My second wife, Rose and I were married in November 1999 at St Patrick's Roman Catholic Church in Brighton, Michigan, her place of worship. We had decided to live in my home in Milford. Rose made St Mary Roman Catholic Church in Milford her place of worship. I continued at Christ Lutheran. At Christ Lutheran's Christmas Eve service Rose was denied participation in communion. I was appalled and so angry that my journey as a Lutheran came to an abrupt end.

I began attending St Mary in Milford with Rose and took part in the sacrament of the Eucharist. I eventually observed that the Catholic tradition forbid my participation which was the unexpressed position of the Lutheran church as well.

Upon discovery, I arranged an appointment with Father Ron Anderson to make my views regarding communion known. To my complete astonishment, I was welcomed to participate in the sacrament of the Eucharist. Now I was on my journey's path with the Catholic tradition.

I felt that I should become a member of the church and entered the R.I.C.A. (Rite of Christian Initiation for Adults) instruction requirement. At the Easter Vigil service in 2007 I became a member of the Roman Catholic Church. It was a memorable service and remains my favorite each year.

Since acceptance my faith journey has accelerated. Continued participation in the Thursday morning men's group of which I was the "token Lutheran" when I was welcomed, Bible study opportunities, and adult formation programs offered by the church have expanded my knowledge, increased my awareness, and provide a continuing path in my journey to discover.

The men's group over the years have discussed books written by widely recognized authors of books and articles of faith, invited pastors of other Christian denominations to speak to us, visited churches, a synagogue, and the most prominent mosque in southeastern Michigan to further our need to discover. Hindu, a religion of India was also presented.

Discussions on religious topics have been spirited and opinions hardly represent a monolithic dogmatic church. To this day I am surprised by the range of thought expressed in our group of usually twenty or so. Remarkable also is the absence of argument. We do not seem to particularly subscribe to all messages from the hierarchy in Rome.

Bible study and adult formation classes have provided mind opening discussion and breathed life into scripture. All has been interesting and educational but nothing has clarified what God has ordained for me. It has been suggested that perhaps I am not listening attentively. My journey of faith continues.

THE INCIDENT

It was early November in the year 1984. I was sitting in my trailer office at 711 Helen Avenue in Detroit when an employee entered and indicated he had lost something that he thought would be at his work station that day.

The main factory lighting had been turned off and together we walked into the area equipped with the huge guillotine like machine used to chop three inch diameter pure copper logs into large nuggets used in the plating industry. The room was totally dark and so I led the way into the room to access the light switch. He stopped at the door and called to me. I turned and strode toward him and was greeted by an explosion.

I knew that I was seriously wounded the nanosecond the bullet entered my chest. As I was driven back by the force into the darkened room perhaps five additional explosions followed. In one corner of the room appeared a dazzling vision, an image which I ponder to this day. The projectile miraculously had been diverted, I was to discover.

Although weakened and shaking I felt no pain. I rose and began a search for a weapon I could use, however useless, and began to examine my alternatives. I needed to find a way to the telephone located in my trailer office. Some time elapsed as I collected myself. Why, I tried to reason, was this happening. Perhaps the recently delivered 20 tons of pure copper had become the incentive for the incident. Armed with a one inch diameter copper rod, I contemplated how I could reach my office. Believing him in the building, I exited the factory through another door, entered the parking lot, and walked toward the trailer one hundred feet away.

The perpetrator was seated in a vehicle outside the gate to the parking lot. He exited the vehicle, entered the lot, and came toward me. Inexplicably he turned, ran to his vehicle, and left the scene. At the time it surprised me that I discovered him to be outside the building. It was clear to me then that he was awaiting the return of my son Stephen with the delivery truck which he would need for transport of the copper.

Slowly and falteringly, totally exhausted I finally reached my trailer office and called 911. In minutes, sirens blaring, police and an emergency response vehicle arrived. The paramedics stabilized me and transported me to Receiving Hospital minutes away. I remember going into x-ray more than once because emergency room personnel could only account for nine entry/exit locations. They needed ten or evidence of a projectile. One of the staff finally discovered an exit wound under my left armpit and I was wheeled to surgery. Whoever was the ER chaplain came to me and asked if I would like him to offer prayer. I did not know until I had been released from recovery how serious an event I had experienced. The chaplain happened upon me later and revealed to me that he was sure I was about to die in that emergency room.

The large scars run the length of my torso which remind me of the trauma. Physical damage was extensive. The bullets had ricocheted throughout my body necessitating the removal of my spleen and a section of my colon. Repaired but in danger of developing peritonitis, a colostomy was performed resulting in an extreme change in my life for several months.

When healed a reconnection procedure was performed and about a week later gas was passed signaling a success. The surgeons at Receiving had accomplished their mission, as had each individual on the team that had kept me breathing.

At the time psychological damage was great as well. Faith in my fellow man was shattered in that instant. My ability to judge a person, a trait I was proud of, was entirely destroyed.

In the twilight of my recovery from the original lifesaving operation, I heard the comforting voices of my wife and ever positive daughter-in- law Pamela. From all the voices in my past, Pam's resonates from the desolate days immediately following this disaster. The words I cannot recall, but the hope and cheer she exuded toward me meant more than all the prayers and wishes for recovery at the time. I remember also words of encouragement from my friend and mentor Gust Jr. who visited often during those early days.

Not the least of the important visits were those of perhaps two or three of my employees. It was their visits that allowed me to begin the healing of the psychological trauma.

At last, home for recovery, I was literally helpless. Fully dependent on a visiting nurse, who arrived occasionally, and my loving spouse who each day changed the dressings on the open wound and provided whatever assistance was required for my colostomy, I continued to heal.

It is difficult to determine how this incident changed me. Physically, after time, I was healed. The support I received from my employees, my family, most importantly my bride when I needed it most, resulted in recovery mentally.

However, I do know that spiritually there was a change. At the time of the incident I could be best described as agnostic. I know now that by the grace of God, I live today. I am confident that I was spared for a purpose. It is a mission that He has chosen not to reveal as yet. I continue to prayerfully wait.

FORGIVENESS - RETRIBUTION - A quandary

Sunday March 6, 2016. Church of the Resurrection Destin, Florida. Father Tom Guido about to deliver the homily. Forgiveness, appropriate for him, astounding for me, was the message. It brought back my most horrific memory.

Father Tom had been assaulted in late November 2015 while walking his dog, Brigitte. A jaw broken in two places, surgeries, and a wired jaw for weeks had totally incapacitated him during Christianity's most beloved holiday. In the homily he admitted difficulty with the concept of forgiveness and had labored long over it, despite his calling as priest.

I realized immediately that I must speak with him. Could I possibly discover a path toward forgiving the individual who totally incapacitated me in 1984?

The horrific event of my life occurred in November 1984 but there is more to relate. I had written to Coleman Young, then mayor of Detroit, and in my anger made a reference to him that one of "his people" had caused the event that nearly took my life. To his credit the mayor responded with a letter telling me in no uncertain terms that "his people" were the 911 operators, police and the paramedics who responded in minutes, stabilized me, and the doctors who attended me at Detroit's Receiving Hospital. I recall that I was surprised by his letter, his offense at my suggestion, and his definition of his people. Four years later I had reason to agree with Coleman Young.

In the spring of 1988 I received a telephone call from the Detroit Police Department asking me if I could come to Rivard Street headquarters to identify a suspect that had been arrested for a crime. With all haste I made the trip from Livonia to downtown Detroit and there he sat, the perpetrator of the event that to this day I have not forgiven him.

In September 1988 the perpetrator went to trial and unbelievably he opted to represent himself. On that day in 1984 while paramedics worked on me, I vaguely recall answering questions for the police. I also know that the investigators discovered evidence at the crime scene. At trial I was astounded that the statements and evidence had been preserved and now appeared in the courtroom.

Mary Hickey, a young white woman, was the prosecuting attorney, a fact I thought would be a disadvantage in presenting the case to a fourteen person jury made up of black Detroiters with the exception of one of Hispanic origin.

Judge Warfield Moore was considered a "hanging" judge by the prosecutor. At the time I felt the cards were stacked against me and justice would be the loser despite the judge's reputation.

At the end of the trial, the defendant as well as I were invited to make a statement to the judge before sentencing. The defendant had recruited a number of persons, all clergy, I was informed, to plead for his position. Not one of these individuals rose to speak after discovery that a guilty of attempted murder verdict had been delivered on their fellow clergy member.

My statement concluded with a reference to two lines from the movie, The Sting. The first had to do with capability. Paul Newman's Gondor asks Hooker, portrayed by Robert Redford, why he wishes revenge for a friend's loss of life through the operation of a confidence game. Hooker replies, "I don't know enough about killing to kill". The parallel in my case was that after the incident retribution was in the hands of the criminal justice system. It was all I knew how to do.

The second line was in response to Gondor's question after the confidence game's success, "Well kid, was it enough?" Hooker replied "It's not enough but it's close". The parallel in my case was that those citizens involved in our criminal justice system had successfully put the sting on the perpetrator. Shortly thereafter, Judge Warfield Moore handed down the sentence. It wasn't enough but it was close.

My conversation with Father Tom ranged from conjecture to reality. He immediately understood my issue and its difficulty and also recognized the difference in intent and severity of our personal experience. At one point he told of an event that resulted in death and yet the families of the parties had found forgiveness and were close. He offered to put me in touch with them in the hope that an earlier statement I had made, that forgiveness was impossible, could be modified. I declined that invitation believing it to be unnecessary.

Upon leaving I told Father that I carried no burden about this issue in my day to day life. . Father Tom's words in response weigh heavily on me today. "Perhaps you have already forgiven the man". Yes... Perhaps!

EPILOGUE

Dear Father Tom

It has been several weeks since our meeting. I found it helpful in my struggle with forgiveness. I am enclosing an essay I prepared and presented to my group of beginning creative writers. I hope the facts and thoughts expressed are accurately portrayed insofar as your incident and struggle.

I have come to a position I do not understand. How can the heart forgive and the mind refuse to accept? The rational mind seems all powerful but is there an understanding? It is a dilemma.

Participation in adult christian formation in two "alpha" sessions has been helpful but not a solution. I have found small discussion groups beneficial. Resurrection sponsored a seminar by Father William Meninger, an advocate and spokesperson for centering prayer. At this seminar we purchased the book "The Process of Forgiveness". I have discovered and read a number of paragraphs to assist and validate my journey.

I am slowly coming to the conclusion you offered; that perhaps I have already forgiven. God knows, I do not.

My favorite psalm is 25. I have just realized that the subheading is entitled "Confident prayer for forgiveness and guidance." It is remarkable how the subject of forgiveness has suddenly become a focus in my life which was brought forward by your homily and your episode with evil.

Perhaps your homily and your

parting words at our meeting will become the most important aid in my struggle as we travel into the future.

Sincerely,
Max Kirschke

THE EVILS OF TOBACCO

TO WHOM IT SHOULD CONCERN: A treatise for youth on cigarette smoking and those who think they have heard it all before.

Smoking filtered cigarettes killed my wife of forty three years and it wasn't from lung cancer.

Recently, memories emotional and painful were brought forward by a series of public information commercials on health focusing on the use of tobacco. Perhaps you have seen them. They recall for me the utter despair of losing a loved one from the often devastating destructive use of tobacco.

I've been told that I'm wasting my time in writing to you. The belief system of youth especially, and most adults as well, do not consider death, much less death from a sometime curable medical condition. One might as well be speaking to the wind, and usually is, when this subject is under discussion. Immortality reigns.

Today I pray that I can make an impact on your current behavior. You will not have to strain your imagination far, for what I have to say is truth.

Make a mental note of the activities you love to engage in and picture the people you love and who love you.

As you light up again, consider which of the activities you would choose to give up because you can no longer breathe without dragging an oxygen cylinder wherever you go.

Perhaps you would rather consider losing a limb or being unable to speak or swallow. It is a decision you should give thought to each time.....but odds are you will not!

I cannot believe you would be indifferent to those you love and love you who will be providing the care you will require. This, of course, is theoretical and may not be the avenue you travel or the heartache you will provide. But consider the probability.....but odds are you will not!

Now ask yourself if merely the thought is abhorrent. Alas! You would rather enjoy another cigarette than have to think about your future as an invalid.

The impact I am hoping to make is that you will gain the strength to make the right decision for you. If you seem hopelessly hooked today, can you accept the probability that your activities and your loves will need to be altered and abandoned?

I have fought through the difficult process of kicking the smoking habit. I also watched and cared for someone who snatched a deadly but curable cancer. I am unforgettably familiar with the condition that renders the smoker unable to speak or swallow.

Imagine breakfast, lunch, and dinner in a bag of liquid nutrient provided through a port in your abdomen. The taste of a Big Mac, a slab of BBQ ribs, your favorite adult beverage just a memory forever.

You are young, in your sixties, full of life, enjoying golf, playing bridge with your friends, looking forward to those golden years when a lump suddenly appears in your mouth. An immediate trip to the dentist, a referral to a specialist, a biopsy, and then the dreaded diagnosis, cancer.

The initial surgery, just five months after the lump was noticed, and just two months after diagnosis, was considered successful by all. The aggressive cancer cells returned with a vengeance and a second procedure had to be performed a few months later. Part of the tongue that triggers the swallowing mechanism was gone. The capability of speech disappeared as well.

Imagine further a spouse or other loving person who cares for you enough to several times per day stimulates the back of your throat with a swab, an exercise intended to eventually restore the swallowing mechanism. You cannot imagine what doing this is like.

Severe pain will be the least of the battles you face. Chemical cocktails designed to arrest and possibly eliminate the dreaded cells will be prescribed and living in a hospital like environment at home must be faced.

All of this happened and came to naught for the lady I loved and cared for to the very, very bitter and painful end.

You feel confident this will never happen to you. Your activities will remain endless, ever growing, and your loves will be forever. Never will there be sadness, mourning, or grieving….at least not for you! But what are your odds?

You have a chance, perhaps greater than half that you can survive the ravages that may set upon you. Perhaps you will be immune to the smell of stale tobacco on your clothing, in your car, and throughout your home. Nonsmokers will notice.

The greatest impact, in helping you decide, could arise if you would consider volunteering a little of your time in a hospital or hospice residence. Perhaps working there would provide incentive to quit this dangerous habit.

Among the patients in hospice will be the younger ones now in their fifties or sixties who decided to continue to light up and enjoy one more. Is smoking cigarettes really worth the clear potential of your disabling and debilitating early death?

IV

The Worst: 1998, The Best: 1999

(215-224)

THE WORST: 1998

It was early January. My love, Bertha Irene had just celebrated number sixty-six. Soon after, Bert finally acquiesced to the probability that chemotherapy would no longer aid in her recovery from the oral cancer she had been fighting so valiantly. It was the most devastating moment of my life.

The impending death of a spouse brings forward a rush of confusing thoughts and emotions. At first there is disbelief. It is as difficult now as it was then to understand the why of such confusion. There is sorrow, guilt, regret, relief all arriving simultaneously. What could have been but now will never be haunts one for a time as well.

The hospital staff moved into action and brought one last teammate into our life. Her name forgotten, her demeanor calm and compassionate, she spoke of hospice care. Arbor Hospice, selected by UofM was instrumental in the weeks until her death and for the months of counseling me. I was pleasantly informed by the hospice investigator that I would qualify as Bert's caretaker and that therefore she could remain living at our home in Milford.

Rather than abandon life, Bert continued to live, participating with friends and family in the activities familiar. The two of us composed an unusual letter which was mailed to all. In that letter we explained the situation and invited all to come to the every Sunday open house where we could share albums of pictures, movies, and memories of brighter days. Not surprisingly our home became a busy location where family, friends, and acquaintances gathered to relive the grand experiences

The most regular visitor was Bert's beloved brother Gust, Jr. I believe she was waiting for a final visit one afternoon. That evening she quietly passed away. I called Arbor Hospice as instructed. They saw to the details. It was February 22, 1998

Grief recovery varies. Some go it alone. I could not. Sharing in a group environment seemed necessary and was important in my recovery. To my rescue also came my brother Bill who called regularly, Al Von Steeg a friend of long standing, who had time for me on occasional visits to his home for talk, Gust Jr. my life long mentor and, most surprising, nephews Mark Kirschke, who called from Houston, Texas, and Alan Headbloom, Gust Jr's son. All played an unexplainable yet important and valuable role.

It was strange moving from a couple's world into a world of unwanted isolation. The coupled persons whom you associated with became invisible. I do not mean this as condemnation. The common thread that kept us together had broken and there was also a need for a time of recovery.

It was Easter Sunday that Alan had invited me to join a small group for dinner at his home in Midland. It was a classic novel like affair in that the guests attending did not know each other and literally brought to the table stories and topics of interest which resulted in spirited conversation. The trip home brought forth an aspiring frame of mind.

In the Summer Bill hosted the first of the Kirschke reunions. Everyone was there and happiness abounded. A "fresh as a daisy" (actually a field of sunflowers) photograph has a prime position on my desk to this day.

Throughout this period were welcome visits to Gust Jr.'s home in Rochester Hills.

By summer's end, grief support had prepared me for reentry into life as it should be. My regular support caller from Arbor, Carolyn, ventured the opinion that perhaps it was time to join a social group of singles of like experience.

September was my first encounter with the "Betweeners", a group of party loving ladies, as I was to discover. One other gentleman attended that first meeting and I believe this fact brought us both back month after month. This group was the final step in my rehabilitation. I had been in jail long enough.

In December at the group Christmas party, coming down the stairs to the party room was a vision who had just returned from an outing in China. Her name was Rose. I immediately felt that I must get to know this vision. At that moment she became more than another active "Betweener".

It took a little time for me to muster the courage to call her and meet with her on a one to one level. Dinner at "Zukies on the Lake" was our first together. I was attempting to get to know her. Rose understood dinner to be about counseling me. It finally dawned on her that she was on a date.

Life had come full circle for me and the story of 1999 began and became the first year of the best years of my life.

THE BEST: 1999

Life had returned to an expectant state. All aspects of my being had become positive as 1998 drew to a close. By the end of this year life will have become nothing short of ecstatic.

I had become a member of the "B'tweeners", that group of fun loving supportive ladies also recovering from the experience of a lifetime. I was thoroughly enjoying the camaraderie that was prevalent and freely offered. They provided far more healing than I expected at the time I was encouraged to join by Arbor Hospice. Among the regularly gathered was a lady named Rose whose presence produced a persistent growing desire and emotion that first manifested itself at the Christmas party in December 1998 and would not diminish.

She had begun to allow me to visit her on occasion. It soon appeared that I could not be out of her presence for any period of time. Sitting home alone, I resorted to writing letters to express my feelings toward her. Often I would call late in the evening after a day's work at Milford Gardens to hopefully hear she would accept company. Even the shortest visit was enough when granted.

A reservation at the SunDial in St. Petersburg Beach in mid-February was on my schedule. The loneliness that was to overcome me was distressful and within a few days I had enough of the Sunshine State and was on my way back. An April Sunday brunch with my adopted group of ladies, A Summer outing in Bay City sailing on a multi masted old pirate ship doing some crewing, my first trip to Stratford's Shakespeare Festival to see stage performances, evening pot luck get-togethers', a trip to Toronto for Phantom, pool parties at Beagan Court and Oak Valley, and a few days at the Grand Hotel on Mackinac Island filled the summer. I drew ever closer to Rose and felt that our relationship was blossoming.

During the summer Rose suggested that I should consider traveling. She had committed to a trip to Switzerland and thought perhaps that there could be an opening if I were interested. I had never traveled nor had a particular interest in doing so. However, my interest in her was overpowering. I inquired, discovered there was a space, and in October we were in Engelberg, Switzerland. But that is another story.

A much more significant episode was on my horizon. With great apprehension one August evening, on bended knee, I proposed to Rose. To an immense disappointing moment her reply was "No! I'm not ready." Since this was not an all or nothing proposal, I begged, still on bended knee, that the relationship could continue. Thankfully, Rose's reply was, "Why not?".

Were there other suitors? It would not have surprised me. It had crossed my mind. Beauty, vivaciousness, intelligence, at any age, are qualities in short supply and highly sought after.

Happy times continued. What seemed like ages later, Rose.somehow provided a signal, at least so I thought, and once more I asked for her hand. Rose responded with YES!

You would not understand how a mid-sixties aged man could say that it was the happiest moment in his life. It was. Marriage was set for some time in 2000 according to church rules or tradition.

Questionnaires had to be completed, children from our marriage had to be raised in the Catholic faith, and there were other conditions that obviously were normally directed to younger first timers. One condition, however, was the necessity of attendance at a pre-marriage retreat for what could be called counseling. It was a valuable experience. Listening to one another without interruption, then repeating what was said before speaking to the problem under discussion, was a lesson for a lifetime.

Then a surprise. We were informed by the parish priest, Father Dan that we would not have to wait the required time before we could marry. November 27, 1999 was open and became our date. With gathered family attending we were joined at St. Patrick's Roman Catholic Church in Brighton, Michigan.

Rose agreed to make Beagan Court, my residence, our home. Much of the details that required attention were resolved during our visit to Switzerland. As a result our honeymoon was a carefree, problem less, ecstatic vacation on Aruba, a small island, not on many maps, just off the coast of Venezuela.

We were together and in love forever. The happiness has never diminished.

V

Essays and Observations

(225-248)

THE GROUP

A seeming truth that had resided in the recesses of the mind was exposed for an instant and brought forth, upon reflection, a torrent of concurring examples. That truth was the power of the group.

Often we all attribute the status we have achieved to our own abilities, enthusiasm, and work ethic without considering the contributions of a particular group of which we have been a member. We have acknowledged parents, teachers, and mentors but rarely, if ever, the dynamics offered within a group. Reflecting upon my own life, suddenly I found what I had failed to acknowledge.

Who or where would I be without the experiences with boyhood buddies, fraternity life, boards of directors, men's clubs, grief support groups, family gatherings, and most currently our group of aspiring creative writers? These have risen to a conscious level immediately. Further examination may bring forth more associations that could loosely be defined as a group.

This revelation is rather sobering. One group after another has helped mold who I am and now I am convinced that who or what I will become will be the result of my participation in future groups of ever changing people.

I am convinced the person that considers himself or herself as a self-made individual has failed to recognize the support received from association with a number of groups.

The Muse Comes Forth

For 67 of my nearly 84 years I knew that I was not a member of that segment of society that classifies itself as creative. Instead I was "concrete sequential", a term Rose on occasion has used in referring to me.

Despite the fact that I have accomplished more than I ever thought I could in the past sixteen years, thanks to Rose's continued insistence that "you can do it", I remained convinced that creativeness was someone else's strength.

Creativeness has slowly evolved and in the nearly two years of participation in creative writing workshops it has become stronger. The inner me, the one I knew did not exist, quite suddenly yearned to be heard and the captive audience of the workshops listened, criticized, and encouraged. Never before had I expressed myself in this manner. I felt rewarded.

That blank sheet of paper that often sits waiting for me to fill with words has drawn out from the recesses of my brain the Muse who has cowered before the concrete sequential bully.

She has helped me to describe the beauty and horror of life and the loveliness of nature that I have witnessed and kept secret.

She has helped me to discover that my life has had many unique experiences that she is sure needs to be related regardless of interest to anyone else.

She has overcome the resident bully in the sequential logic oriented half of my brain.

She has allowed a forceful gale to enter and further extend the boundaries of creativity. This wind suggests that I am capable if only I will permit myself to explore. My Muse jumps for joy as I enthusiastically embark in previously unimagined creative endeavors.

New associations usually lead an individual into new and different activities. The past seventeen years with my Rose, the recent two with Susan, and today with Gail have created the renewed me to the pleasure of my Muse.

What will tomorrow reveal? The thought excites my being. My Muse awaits expectantly.

STRATFORD

It is most enjoyable and always interesting to get away from the ordinary day to day…even for a short time. Sharing a phenomenal meal with persons one has never met and unlikely to ever be in their presence again is an exhilarating experience.

Rose and I have for a number of years traveled to the theatre town of Stratford just eighty-eight miles east of the Port Huron Blue Water Bridge. There during the afternoon and evening we enjoy what live theatre presents, and when not at theatre, strolling the West bank of the Avon exulting in the quietude in the company of swans and mobs of ducks that gather in expectation of handouts of corn. Stratford is a welcoming city and for us the meticulously manicured gardens add to our pleasure.

Breakfast, however, is the event that makes our trip so special. Our hosts, Victoria and Murray Sanderson, who own and operate Mornington Rose provide the environment beginning at 8:00a.m. with coffee at the sideboard in the dining room which we leisurely consume in the adjoining parlor. As the usually eight guests appear introductions are made and conversations begun until Murray announces the menu and places it on the sideboard signaling that breakfast will be served momentarily.

The breakfasts are without exception culinary creations perhaps more ingenuous than anything served in a so called upscale establishment. Choice of juices comes before a parfait concoction set off with a floral delight from their herb garden.

Imagine French toast cut from a baguette with sautéed bananas and a light syrup atop, or a quiche served in a ramekin. Potato, bacon, sausage, a small amount of very finely chopped greens and other ingredients are offered at breakfast. In between the courses we may sample Murray's fresh baked scones. The menu varies, the presentation always impeccable, the taste to savor rather than hungrily consume the company gregarious. That is the Mornington Rose experience.

At last and promptly at 9:00a.m. we are invited to the table. Conversations begun continue, and most often change to other subjects, as Murray begins to serve and we discover a little more of everyone. Rose and I long ago learned at this table how very different each of us are, that our paths are diverse beyond expectations, and that each of us has a unique story that encompasses our lives. How blessedly different we are outside of our visible touchable humanness. It would be impossible to learn about another human being over a two hour gathering in the morning at a bed and breakfast but what is revealed is always interesting, informative, and often educational.

Most often the encounter leaves one wanting to know more of an individual but the moment has expired. Life now continues along the path now traveled. Rose and I relish these brief encounters.

All are invited to provide a comment in the Mornington Rose diary prior to leaving the breakfast table. It is difficult to verbalize the extraordinary.

A short sidebar on Stratford and Mornington Rose: The theatre performances are generally superb, and importantly at night, upon return to Mornington Rose: there are Murray made chocolate chip cookies and a bucket of ice for that goodnight cocktail.

SECOND MARRIAGES

UNPARALLELED EXPERIENCES

Marriage is a complicated state of being with many external factors arising that influence this sacred relationship. One of those factors, for later in life second marriages, is the family that each brings to the table.

Rose and I became a onesome among fifty family members gathered at Saint Patrick's Roman Catholic Church in Brighton. A marriage just a bit over and a bit under two years after the death of our spouses. That could have been considered too soon by members of the respective families. If so, it was never verbalized by either. I am sure that Rose's sons and daughters and my sons as well applauded our union without reservation. Rose's oldest daughter, Laura, and my brother Bill attended us at the Alter and Bryan, her oldest son, offered the toast for our happiness at the reception Rose had arranged at Baker's of Milford.

I had never experienced the joys found in a father daughter relationship so I welcomed this late arriving event. I have grown to love the experience with Rose's four daughters. I missed their early years but as adult women, I have witnessed and applauded the extraordinary growth and diversity of their lives. I could not be prouder of their accomplishments as wives, mothers, and women.

Five of our twenty-eight grandchildren have been born since Rose and I began seeing each other. Two granddaughters, one seventeen, the other soon to be, one grandson, a little younger and most recently, since February 2005, twin girls. None have been hooked on today's electronic wireless devices, preferring to be actively involved in life as were their now twenty three older cousins.

Nikki and husband Chris have four, all born after our marriage delivered while we waited along with Ray and Karin Horn, Chris's parents in the hospital lobby birthing area. The birth of the twins, April and Ella, provided a unique experience in my life.

In years long ago, even as father, there was little connection to the newborn. The doctor entered the waiting room, provided the announcement, commented briefly, and retired through the door he entered. We were fortunate to see the wife and newborn hours after they had been comfortably placed in a room and nursery. Often, the child could only be viewed through a glass barrier sometimes held, if you were lucky, by the attending nurse.

Nikki had welcomed me to witness the twins growth while they remained yet unborn. My first experience of viewing a child's development through an ongoing ultrasound session was unbelievably exciting and awe inspiring. At the time, and even today, the invitation to attend this very intimate procedure was stunning.

Being able to connect with the girls, however remotely, only heightened the tremendous joy of holding April and Ella very shortly after their birth. Wrapped in a small blanket and wearing a warm hat, each seemed barely larger than the palm of my hand. The pleasure of possessing a newborn granddaughter even for a short moment is miraculous. Emotion overcomes.

In my seventies at the time, I was unprepared for such an experience. The years have gone by but I still recall the pleasure of being with them at their home holding and changing, feeding and occasionally comforting them. Nikki and Chris somehow knew how important this was. At least for this grandfather.

My daughters, heart adopted, have provided the kind of experiences one cannot achieve from sons. I will always be grateful for the many times they have shown that they care for me.

FATHER AND SONS

The relationships between father and sons is difficult one to relate, at least for this father. Charles in 1956, Stephen in 1958, and Eric in 1961, each brought joy at their birth and continued as they grew from youngsters to young adults. As they now reach middle age, each is beyond fifty, they remain a joy for me.

It has been an opinion I have held that the men in a marital relationship gravitate to their spouses' family and culture and so a decided reduction in contact is inevitable. So it was and is in my life. Nevertheless it does not affect the bond that was created in earlier life. I continue to love and respect the persons they have become and I believe that that feeling for me exists in each one. At my advanced age I am comfortable that I performed my obligation as a father.

Early in their lives, they recognized their parent's desire for them to do well in school both academically and in citizenship. They were encouraged to participate in the lives of their peers. All three became involved in competitive swimming for several years and each brought unforgettable memories to me. Their accomplishments, acknowledged by ribbons and medals, important to them at the time, are inconsequential when compared to the character traits instilled at home and nurtured by Gordon Larson, their high school math teacher by day, demanding competitive swim coach evenings. He played an indispensable role in their development as young men. Never give up, persevere, do your best, applaud your competitor, work hard are among the valuable lessons of life learned and reinforced pool side.

Upon graduation from Clarenceville High swim scholarships were offered to Charles and Stephen for outstanding performance in their specialty by Central Michigan University. Eric, burned out after ten years of competition, also enrolled at Central Michigan upon graduation. Charles and Eric progressed through the university workload and graduated. Steve was another story.

I recall that he came home following his freshman year with the statement that he did not wish to continue his education. For lack of a positive alternative, his mother and I insisted that he must return. Being one of our perfect sons he returned for his sophomore year. At the completion he returned with the same desire. This time he announced a positive alternative. His desire was to enter the work a day world as one of my employees. That relationship had its problems and rewards and that is another chapter in the book of life.

I view my sons as successful human beings. I am very proud of them. My hope is that they view themselves in the same manner.

THE GAZEBO

For a number of years the ugly mound of sand, rocks, and weeds just eighty feet south of the west end of our home was looked at with disgust by me but not without a dream… a dream of a structure surrounded in beauty. My Rose continually prompted me, but ever so casually, to realize this dream. As I stood on top of that nondescript pile looking about and down on the gardens that we had begun, it slowly dawned upon me to prepare a plan of conversion rather than continue with frustration and sometime anger.

Shortly after attending a home and garden exposition at the Pontiac Silver Dome one year, where I had seen a magnificent gazebo displayed, Rose and I went to the manufacturer of the structure whose factory was located in the city of Milford. We decided on a model and soon after I began sinking the pylons that were to support the floor. It wasn't long before we picked up the floor components and amazingly discovered that I had accomplished the initial phase with surprising accuracy. The corners of the gazebo floor rested on the pylons and the floor was level. The walls were next and were erected quickly and without incident. The roof was another story and without the assistance provided by son-in-law Lynn Giese and the owners of Gazeboes, Inc., we wouldn't have what we have.

The structure was finished in a soft honey brown tinted stain and then the screens installed. All that remained were the table and chairs which came soon after. A shallow boulder filled ravine on the north side of the gazebo allowed a stairway to nowhere that added structure to the landscape.

The four steps to the paver floor bring into unrivaled focus the row of strawberry hewed daylilies and from there a view of our resident giraffe, majestically peering over the veldt surrounding him, admiring the view in his stony vision. Gardens on all sides of our grand gazebo were devised and completed over several seasons and now the plantings and landscape, mature in their beauty, beyond our expectations, provide the essence, the reality of what I had envisioned.

An artist's pallet of wondrous Iris shades, the deep purple globe shaped and wild looking alliums arrive in the spring. In summer, the fragrance of phlox and Asian lilies, the greens blues and gold leaves of the hosta, the purple leaves and gold flower clusters of the ligularia, and so much more all arrive in their time and provide unmatchable pleasure. Even in autumn the chocolate jopi, the improbable toad lilly and the ever present chrysthemum exhibit their loveliness. During all seasons, Rose and I often reside with crystal goblets of pinot noir in the wane of day and view what God has wrought and make plans for tomorrow.

The olive colored metal framed arm chairs revolve and with little effort we can view our land, some of it beautiful, some of it not so. We thoroughly enjoy being in our little get away place.

The scenes have inspired me to take untitled thoughts of whatever subject currently of interest to me and record them as "A view from the gazebo". I have concluded that the phrase best describes my ruminations.

The exercise of recording memoir these past months has given me much pleasure. It now demands me to occasionally record my observation and feelings about events of the day that interest me. Concurrence or rejection of what I pen matters not. It is I.

R & M Truffle Time

The nearly black chocolate melts ever so slowly in the family sized double boiler on the kitchen stove. Mustn't get a drop of water into the brew that is about to become ganache, that soft center of the truffle that provides an aroma and taste so heavenly it is difficult to describe…no impossible! It is told that just a small drop of water will ruin the batch and so great vigilance and patience are exerted.

Long before the melt, the exercise begins with the order and delivery of the deeply flavored semi sweet block of Peter's Burgundy chocolate, the perfect choice for our incomparable product.

When it arrives with the chocolate destined for the molds, preparation for the conversion of the kitchen to a truffle producing establishment begins.

Bring out the molds, plain and fancy, assure their condition, make space in freezer and fridge, clear the counters. Bring out the pans, the pastry tubes and paraphernalia. Check for the flavor ingredients. Purchase the nuts, the heavy cream and egg nog. We need cocoa, coconut to toast, maraschino cherries and cream cheese. What have we forgotten?

Rediscover the secret recipes. Carefully measure the burgundy chocolate as prescribed and place the portion aside. Each will provide forty-five of the delectable creations.

Melt the chocolate for the molds and fill the cavities to the rim. Shortly then, empty the cavities of their contents. Remaining and hardening is the conventional dome of the most delicious confection known to the lover of chocolate. Trays of truffle domes rest waiting to be filled with ganache that reveals aroma and taste of rum and egg nog, or raspberry, or amaretto all of which have been thoroughly sampled before the pour into the pastry tube.

Ganache, soft enough for the pastry tube, solid enough to roll, prepared from the secret recipes now comes forth. The domes are filled and the truffles that prefer to be rolled are soon in bite sized balls.

Another application of chocolate to seal in the exquisite tastes. Then, into the freezer, and after a time out they come, are popped from their cavities, and then rest expectantly waiting to be identified with colorful little dots or squiggly lines.

I often hope for a failure or two, a truffle unfit to exhibit.

Finally the colorfully decorated, the varied shapes, and the bite sized balls are placed with loving care into their holiday paper cups and put into shiny white boxes tied with a ribbon or metal tins decorated with Christmas and winter scenes.

Family, friends, and neighbors will soon receive their intended package.

Care for an **R & M Truffle** anyone?

'TIS THE SEASON

Mid November and once more festive thoughts of past holidays begin to enter our consciousness. For Rose and me, Thanksgiving to Christmas has always been the season, a special time to celebrate family.

In the first year or two of first marriages, the celebration of the season was with our spouse. Then came the children and celebrations became even more joyful. Rose and I have come full circle and once again we celebrate for the two of us. Most of the seasons delight, however, lives in the recall of fond memories.

Our children, who provided the joy of the season, have grown to adulthood, married, begun their families, and have their own traditions. Joy for us now arrives when their children appear at our door or when the families are gathered for the important holiday feasts.

Sadly the feasts are no longer planned by Rose and me, nor are they hosted at our home. Thankfully this labor of love has been handed down, so to speak. Those that brought us such joy years ago now plan and host. Rose and I have become invited guests…honored to be sure, but guests just the same. It feels somehow different but the love and joy remain and are reinforced.

Nevertheless, our holiday preparations have continued on a somewhat smaller scale, but the memories recalled invite us to exert the effort and once again relive the bygone holiday seasons.

Our Christmas tree is brought from its eleven month hiding place and erected and trimmed the Sunday after Thanksgiving. It is embellished with golden lamps and colorful ornaments. Rum and eggnog consumed during the decorating make it easier to judge its completed beauty. Our very special little Christmas tree adorned with mementos of our travels hangs on a wall in another room. The Venetian blown glass gondola poled by Santa, the Russian carved wood Santa Claus, the tiny Belgian lace doily, and many others on the tree revive pleasant memories of our life.

Snowflakes dangle on invisible fishing line accenting our windows, twinkling as the morning sun rises. In the evening icicle lights draping from the gazebo roof and Christmas lights on the rails of our deck make their contribution. All brighten our spirits each day.

One more time Rose and I will savor the aroma and taste of dark semi-sweet chocolate when our kitchen becomes a truffle making factory for a few days. Fifty dozen of our creations will be distributed in holiday tins and sample boxes to family, friends, and neighbors. We will take advantage of the hymns and homilies offered during the season. We will offer prayers of thanksgiving and ask for blessings upon family for the year to come. Then, at last, after dinner on Christmas day we will join in the family white elephant gift exchange. The event brings forth gales of laughter and hooting from the gathered as the mystery gifts are ceremoniously unwrapped. Once again we will experience and commit to memory another joyous season.

Gail Koch

Gail's Tales

Gail's Biography

Grab a cup of coffee, and find a comfy spot, Gail wants to share some stories with you. Her inspiration to write was to get some of the "brain floss" of great memories out of her head and on to paper.

Growing up in the country of northern Michigan during the '40s and '50s, little did she know where her life adventures would take her. She has a passion for creativity, art and travel. She has many stories to tell. They are moments in time, with life lessons and humor. Enjoy.

Dedicated to Bob, my one true love,

Kathi, our precious daughter.

and in memory of our loving son, Ronnie.

Hugs and kisses.

Acknowledgements

My thank you's are my blessing. Bob, my husband of forever, I couldn't have done this without all your help, typing, reading, re-reading, and encouragement. Kathi, our daughter, who inspired me to write stories and help edit the brain floss. More blessings. To family and friends, who rolled their eyes when they read my stories. More blessings. Thanks to my teacher Susan McCoy, classmates, Max Kirschke, Barb Armstrong, and Marty Dooling, who cheered me on. More blessings. To my Beta readers, Peggy Trabalka, Gayle Lafferty, and Karhi Budka. More blessings. And Jim Gunning and Bobby Fenrich for all their help. Last, but not least, thank you God for all my second chances. I am ever so grateful.

Contents

Gails Tales 251

1.

Jump rope

&

Cracker-jacks

The Old Barn

Take my hand, I want to tell you a tale of the old barn. It was built in 1880 with loving hands by friends and neighbors for my great-grandfather Luke.

In 1943, I met the old barn. I was 4 years old. It was home to many cows, pigs, horses, cats, and lots of barn swallows. It was always a thrill to go to the barn to meet a new calf, a bunch of small pink piglets, and many litters of kittens.

As time went by the horses were replaced by a brand new and bright green John Deere Model B tractor. And one by one the rest of the barn animals found new homes.

Playing in the hay was one of my favorite things to do in the barn. Many fun times I had jumping in the hay and even having sleepovers in the haymow. Although, in the morning we smelled so bad from the hay, my mother had to hose us down outside before we were allowed back in the house.

Years have gone by and a toll was taken on the old barn. One too many snowflakes fell on it in November 2014 and the roof fell in. Maybe we can find someone interested in some vintage barn wood to repurpose it for furniture or other home décor. It would be great to extend the life and legacy of the Old Barn.

The Telephone

Hop on the round blue stool with me. We need to call Aunt Elaine and ask her if she would please bring home some 'Double Bubble Gum' because I need it.

It's 1945 and my Aunt Elaine is the local telephone operator. I'm only 6 years old and I don't drive yet so I can't get the gum myself. I can feel the pucker in my mouth and taste the sweetness. Yum!

I stand on my tippy toes on the stool and put the receiver to my ear. I turn the crank on the right side of the phone one time and now I'm ready to talk into the long speaker. I'm so excited! I ask Aunt Elaine to please bring me some gum on her way home from work and she says "Yes!" When I say goodbye, I'm ecstatic but I must remember to hang up the receiver.

This wall telephone is in my Grandma's living room. She lives downstairs. My family lives in the same house, only we live upstairs. A few years later, we get our own phone. It's a desk model, with a smaller black speaker, and on a post with the receiver on the right side. The bell box is on the wall. How cute is that? We are so classy.

One day my Mom was painting the kitchen and painted the bell box to match. It looked really nice but for four days we got no calls. Why? Mom had painted the bells shut.

Our first phone number was 2112. In phone language that's a long, two shorts and a long. With a party line, one had to learn patience because the phone rang a lot but it wasn't always for you.

I Hear a Whistle Blowing

I hear a whistle blowing and I must run. The train is coming!

Growing up on a farm in northern Michigan, the railroad tracks ran right through our property. In 1945, that railroad was the Manistee & Northeastern. The train, nicknamed Maude, ran daily from Traverse City to Northport and back. Northbound, the whistle would blow just before it crossed highway M22. That was my warning. I would drop what I was doing to run up the small hill so I could wave to the engineer. When he saw me, he would always wave back and blow the whistle again. That was the thrill for my day!

If I had been gathering eggs, I had to be very careful running with a basket of fresh eggs. Now if I was in the house and heard the whistle, I had to run outside on the porch. We lived on the second floor of the old farmhouse so I could see the train from this upper level porch. When he blew the whistle, I felt so special. As a kid, I felt like he blew the whistle just for me! When I got older, I realized he was probably blowing his whistle for the road just north of our property. Oh well. In my young heart his waves were just for me. Many times I would blow kisses at the train. It passed by our farm every day for so many years.

In 1970, on one of its last runs, it dropped off a boxcar loaded with steel roofing for our new big barn. How special was that? We had our very own train stop that day!

The train and track have been gone for many years. The old roadbed is overgrown with a thicket of trees and bramble. But every once in a while, I stop there and blow kisses in the wind for a wonderful memory of childhood.

My Playhouse

Strange, how things happen in life. Sometimes we win and sometimes we lose. In 1945 when I was six years old, my Mom was pregnant. We were going to have a new baby. But things went very badly and the baby was stillborn. With deep sadness in their hearts from this loss, my parents clung really tight to me. To cope with this tragedy, they got the idea to build me a real life-sized playhouse.

So with hammer, nails, wood, and a plan, they went to work to build my playhouse. It made me feel very special. A playhouse of my very own. No one I knew had a playhouse outside. And one that looked like their real house!

It was about 4' ft x 6'ft, and with a peak in the roof. It was big enough that you could stand up in it. Mom painted the inside walls blue, trimmed with a flowered wallpaper border. White sheer curtains hung on the windows. It was so pretty and homey! There was a kid sized metal stove, fridge and sink. These sat on orange crates to raise them to my height. There was also enough room for a wooden table and two chairs. The outside was painted white with pink shutters.

So now, let's play house. Here is a box of dress-up clothes. Do you want the blue flowery dress or can I have it? Black high heels are so cool – but it's kind of hard to walk in the grass. Let's look in the box for a big hat and maybe some gloves. You look so darling in your orange dress and white wedge shoes. Doesn't that veil on the hat bug you? We are both looking so stylish. Let's have a cup of tea, or maybe Mom will let us have lunch out here. Mom makes us p.b. & j. sandwiches cut up really small, Ritz crackers with a bit of American cheese on them, along with milk and chocolate chip cookies. What a fancy meal to have in our little house!

It's after lunch now. Let's be mommies. We run inside to get our dolls and their clothes. You had better put a jacket on the baby because it's getting cooler outside. Or just put her in the buggy with a blanket on – she'll be fine.

It's been a long day, playing and pretending. How we should dress, what correct words we should say, and how to take care of our baby dolls. It ends when we have to come back to the real world as Mom calls out – "Come in the house Gail, and set the table for dinner".

I had a fun time today with you. Let's do it again tomorrow!

Wax Paper

The seven mile bus ride to school every day was always my time to day dream. When I hear the bus go up the hilly road near my house to pick up the kids before my stop that was my alarm to dash out of the house. I would run to the corner and be there for it when it came back down the hill. I'd hop on the bus and say good morning to our driver, Mr. Russell. Then go and find a seat.

I stare out the window and review in my mind - did I bring all I need for school? If the weather is nice today, I will bring my roller skates for recess. They are metal clip-ons with leather straps. And I must not forget my skate key. I share my skates with a friend, so I will need the key to adjust them. I check for the blue ribbon around my neck to make sure the key is there. The sidewalk in front of school was in the shape of a "D," hence the name "The Big D." This is where we skate.

Oh! And most importantly, I must also bring a clean sheet of wax paper. It has to be the perfect size, about 15" inches long. Our school has an amazing feature. It has an outside fire escape in the form of a long metal tube. It is about 3' feet wide and 4' feet high in an oval shape. It is a fire exit from the study hall/library on the second floor. At recess and lunch time the teachers would guard this like a hawk because we kids liked to slide down it. But after school, it was fair game.

The challenge was to walk up the inside of this tube. Now here is where you need the *clean* wax paper. If you used one from your lunch, you might get peanut butter on your tidy–whiteys. Not good! So, with your wax paper in your teeth, you carefully climb up the inside of the tube. You crawl up on all fours, feet placed on an angle for less slippage and hands stabilizing. Go up as far as you dare go, because it is dark and scary inside. Then, as quickly as you can, rotate and transfer the wax paper from your mouth to your bum. Sit on it and down you go. Wheeee…that was a great thrill! This ride down the tube was well worth it.

No more day dreaming - I'm at school now. Gotta' go. Thank goodness I didn't forget my piece of wax paper!

2.

Heart

&

Soul

A Lap Dance from Mandy

"Meow, meow, meow," Mandy says to me as she is sitting in the middle of the kitchen floor. In cat to Gail language, that means "sit down in the brown chair so I can sit on you." So I go sit down and she follows with a look in her eyes that says "I'm coming for a lap dance."

She hops on the chair arm, puts her front paws on my leg and waits for me to stroke her head, back, and tail. She likes this and starts to purr. Then she gets her whole body on me. Face to face, she rubs her cheek on the frame of my glasses. Then her wet nose is rubbed on mine. It's like a kitty kiss – a love connection between us. Mandy is marking her territory on me so other kitties will know I'm all hers. Now the purring gets very loud. I love her so.

Next, she kicks her feet out and flops on her back in my lap facing you with her paws up. I am now holding her like a baby. Purr, purr, purr.

With her front paws, she kneads on the right side of my face. Kneading is when kittens want to start their mommy's milk to flow when they are nursing, something she never forgot. She presses her paws left, right, left, right, etc. for some time. It's a real bonding experience. Purr, purr, purr.

I pet her, then scratch gently behind her ears. I run my finger on her cute nose wondering how every hair on her face is so perfect. I even play with her whiskers.

When she is done with this lap dance, she gives a soft meow, gently bites my finger, stands up, jumps down, and walks away with her tail held high. The lap dance is over and we both feel well loved.

Heel Strike

"Gail, today you are going to try to get 'heel strike'" said my therapist. "Heel strike" is when you make a step with your foot and your heel strikes the floor first. This is how it is normal to walk. I try with every fiber in my body to do this, but my toes go down first on every carefully planted step. Learning to walk again at age 56, after a bad bout with Guillain-Barre' Syndrome, is one of my many challenges.

I call Guillain-Barre' Syndrome, or GBS, my trip to Hell and back. It all started with a bout of laryngitis after which my immune system did not shut off and attacked my nerve system. It nibbled its way through the myelin sheath that covers my nerves and had a feast on them. The result was my being paralyzed from the neck down. The trip to the hospital ER confirmed it.

They gave me plasmapheresis (blood filtering) and IVIG (an IV injection of other people's antibodies.) I spent fourteen days in ICU in extreme pain, until I finally was well enough to be rolled down to a step-down unit. I was very lucky that I did not require a breathing machine. Many GBS patients do.

My neurologist came in and said "therapy, therapy, therapy and you will be fine." Now here I lay, flat as a fritter. I can't close my eyes so the nurse tapes them shut at night. To call for help, I must blow into a specially placed tube because I can't move my head or anything else. I couldn't even talk normal. I sounded like Elmer Fudd because my mouth was partially paralyzed.

Rounds of doctors come by and after a bunch of EMG (electromyogram) nerve tests said I probably wouldn't walk again. And my thoughts are "I going to prove you wrong." I wasn't going to let GBS beat me. A quote from John Wayne came to mind about courage "When you are scared to death, you saddle up and ride."

The first time sitting up was 3 ½ seconds. WOW!!! Was I proud. This was going to be a real challenge. Be brave Gail, God will give you strength.

After four and a half months in the hospital, I came home in a wheelchair. I could not walk. The real challenge was learning to walk without the use of my arms. "Heel strike, heel strike," where are you? Finally, one day, I did it! Walking without the fear of falling was hard to overcome. Hands, hands, where are you? You need to be feeding me, washing and wiping me. You need to come back! I pray to be Gail again. She needs to paint pretty pictures and hug people. Oh look, my little finger moved a little bit! It has been seven months since my hands moved at all. Nerves grow back about a millimeter a day, so it takes a long time to reconnect.

Nineteen months of therapy, and many stories to tell. After all of it though, I'm back to me…back to walking, painting and living. Thank you God for putting me back together.

Giggles from the Girdle

Vanity plays a large role in female's lives starting very early. Magazines, TV and media everywhere inspire us to be the perfect size 2. There are many tools on the market to give us the perfect shape. The latest is *Spanx*. They are like an elastic sleeve that you put on over your midsection. My first reaction as I look at it on the hanger is "Holy Moly, you want me to squeeze all this inside that?!" OK, let's give it a shot. Put your legs in the holes on the bottom, and carefully pull up. Well, the crotch is only at my knees and I'm tired out already. After a lot more huffing and puffing I'm finally in them. Now the spare tire roll around my tummy is in my boobs. Wow, I have just gained two bra sizes and the cleavage is bodacious! I am looking like a movie star.

I bend over, mostly to see if I actually can and accidentally pass a bit of gas. My butt cheeks are so tight inside the *Spanx* that what started out as a rumble is now just a mere squeak at the middle of my back. I start to giggle, but choke it back a little because there are other people in the dressing room.

Girdles, or corsets, have been around for years and years. While moving my mother-in-law out of her longtime home in Detroit, I found a real treasure. It was a 1939 Sears & Roebuck catalog. There are thirteen pages of all kinds of girdles and corsets with buttons and hooks that snap, crackle and pop. They are all to make your spare tire or tummy go somewhere else. We all would like to take our tummies off and hang them in a closet on the days we want to look great. That's not possible, so we must girdle it up, and swear we will never have another chocolate chip cookie or hot fudge sundae. But that commitment lasts only until the next day when we let it all hang out again.

Let's go back to the now time. I've got to get out of these *Spanx*! I roll them down to my waist, and then carefully roll them over my rump. Bend over, and Oh,Oh - there goes that gas leak again. Must exit fast. Now, how fast can you run with your *Spanx* at your ankles? Giggles from the Girdle.

Three Gals and a Chevelle

This story is about three classy gals and a 1970 Chevelle. My mother Annette is Gal No. 1. She bought this Chevelle in 1970, brand new, in Traverse City, Michigan. It was light yellow with a black vinyl top, a black interior, and a 307 V8 engine. She loved this car, and always told us "It was the best." Anything she had was always "the best." One kooky thing she did to the car was put daisy bathtub stickers on the hubcaps.

In 1985, I needed a better car to drive and my mother was ready to let the Chevelle go. So she gave it to me. I am now Gal No. 2. It was a great car to drive, with lots of room for our daughter and friends. When she was fifteen and got her drivers permit, the Chevelle was perfect for her to learn in. One Friday night, she and her friend wanted to go "cruise." So we three got all dolled up to go "cruisin." The Chevelle had a bench seat in the front. My daughter would drive and her friend rode shotgun (right seat), and I was in the middle. Part of my attire was a baseball cap, which I would pull down while cruising to disguise my age. The guys would drive by, checking us out, and would want our phone numbers. They would flirt a bit and say no. Then the guys would ask for the phone number for the girl in the middle. My daughter would always answer, "Oh, she's wasted, and sleeping it off."

In 1988, I got another car so I gave the Chevelle to our daughter – she is now Gal No. 3. She had big ideas to restore this car – which by now was 18 years old. With her earnings from her summer job, she started buying parts from everywhere. The fenders came from California. The camshaft came from

Ohio. We went to a local junkyard and bought a 350 small block engine. The oilier the better, because you know how it failed. Her Dad came home from work one day to see an old engine on an engine stand with seven of her gearhead guy friends waiting to hear what her Dad was going to say about this. After the first reaction, which was "holy shit, what's going on?!" she asked him to help her re-build this engine for her car. It was a great bonding project for both of them. About a month later they had the old engine out and rebuilt one in. Without the exhaust pipes on, she started it up. The noise blew the dishes off the shelf! She took it for a brief ride and got a police escort home. Time to buy an exhaust system!

For high school graduation, she wanted fancy 5 star rims and new tires. She worked that summer, made more money, and had the car painted metallic burgundy. She named her car "Little Miss Dangerous." It was a real beauty.

Later, she drove to the dragway to participate in drag races. In one of the races, she beat the guy next to her. He was so pissed-off that a girl had beaten him; he spun through the pit area, put his car on the trailer, and stormed off.

She drove her car daily to college for a couple of years. One day she went to class for a one hour test and when she came out of class, her car was gone. It was never seen again. And thus ended the story of the three classy gals and their Chevelle.

Ronnie See, Ronnie Do

Ronnie, our grandson, was 4 years old in 2006. He was the quiet one, so in the evening his parents would review the alphabet with his wooden blocks. Ronnie would try to say the letters as they were shown to him. This was all the talk you would get from him. He knew his letters well. This turned out to be very important.

On a warm fall day Ronnie was riding home in Mom's car from a long day at pre-school. He was all safely buckled up sleeping in his car seat in the back. On arriving home, Mom stops in the driveway, clicks open the garage door, puts the car in park, and gets out to check the mailbox.

In a flash, Ronnie gets out of his car seat, climbs over the front seat, and puts the gearshift into "D" (drive) just like Mommy. "Ronnie see, Ronnie do."

The car now starts moving towards the open garage door, with Dad's classic car inside. Mom is horrified as she runs back toward the car, only to hear the automatic door lock click shut. She jumps on the running board, as Ronnie is steering. She is shouting at him through the closed window to put the shifter in P. "PUT IT IN P!"

Well, Ronnie puts it in R (Reverse.) Now, the car is reversing heading back towards the street. There is more shouting now. "PUT IT IN P!" So Ronnie puts it in D again, now going slowly into the garage. Thank goodness his Dad, just the night before, had stacked 4 tires at the back wall of the garage. The car stopped when it hit them. All this time, Mommy had been riding the running board, going back and forth.

Now, Ronnie is so scared and he is crying. Mom is still shouting at him and pointing at the window. "Push 'U' to unlock the door!" Ronnie scores on this one, hitting "U" to open the door. Mommy reaches in and shuts the car off. By now, both Ronnie and Mommy were sobbing. She hugged and kissed him. What a frantic few seconds that was. After this episode, our daughter called us and said she needed a beer or a shot, or maybe both.

That night Ronnie and his older brother Scott, who was 6, got a talking to from their dad about waiting until they were older before they tried to drive. No more "Ronnie see, Ronnie do."

3.

Ramblin'

&

Scramblin'

Pampers and Oil

The year was 1971 and it was a new chapter in our life as a couple. I had just given birth to our daughter. She was a wee little one at only 4 ½ lbs. This baby was part of us, and we must plant the seed of adventure in her soul. So we planned a trip to California for September. She would be about 12 lbs. by then.

Bob made a wedge of wood and I padded it with fabric to fit between the bucket seats, as this was a sports car. I bought a snap bed from Farmer Jacks. It was a padded box with mattress about 16"x32" and snaps on corners that folded down when we didn't need it. Perfect! Don't forget the small fabric bouncy chair. Now we are packed and ready to go.

Our gray sports car has 160,000 miles on it. It still purrs like a kitten, but likes to drink oil. This meant that on our journey we would have to make regular stops to buy oil and Pampers, both for "leaks". Our car had a small trunk, but being that it was a convertible there was extra storage where the top stored when it was down.

Warming baby milk was a snap; just put it on the defroster, then keep rolling the bottle. Traveling in small areas can be a bit of a challenge, with feeding, burping, tooting, number 1 & 2 and crying.

In restaurants our daughter would often squeal and fuss, so we ate mostly in drive-ins. At night in motels, I would put our daughter in her snap bed in the bathroom because she always seemed to have a squeaky booger in her nose. But, all in all she was a great traveler.

We were gone a month and saw many sights - the Grand Canyon, Death Valley, friends in California and much more. On a train trip in Colorado, she was the youngest patron on board.

It was a great adventure bonding as a new family. We went through 7 cases of pampers and 98 quarts of oil in a 1960 Corvette.

29 Beers to Alice

In 1972 we board a train called "The Ghan" in Adelaide, Australia for our journey to Alice Springs, a trip of about 1000 miles and 30 hours. The route is through the barren outback desert, where the earth is nothing but red bull-dust, and gravel. Our compartment is so tiny with bunk-beds, the top one a pull-down with a sink/table combo and private toilet. The shower was down the hall. What an experience that was, having a hot shower on a moving train!

The most entertaining place was the lounge car. My attention was on a gold miner. He had already put down 15 beers as I was quietly counting. How big a bladder does he have? Well, we travel along and more beer was served, and he would just smile and talk a bit louder. A few more beers and it was time for dinner in the diner. This chap was so drunk; he stumbled to the diner and sat down. The diner was outfitted to the nines with white linen tablecloths and napkins, china and glassware. The first thing on the table was soup. He had no idea where on his face his open mouth was. At our table sat an aborigine woman who had traveled to Adelaide for surgery and was returning home. She was not familiar with silverware, and was challenged to use them.

After dinner and back in the lounge car, Mr. Gold Miner had a few more beers. With a full tummy he was soon snoring in his chair. We went back to our private berth and snuggled in our bed. The ride over the rails was a bit bumpy and jerky, but it lulled us to sleep.

The next day, we arrived in Alice Springs, a thriving outback town in the middle of the desert. Bob ran up to the front of the train to photograph the engine. Now, what we should have immediately done was go buy a ticket on the return train. But in the few minutes it took for the photos, the ticket office had sold all the tickets. So much for the train ride back.

The next leg of the trip was in a small plane, with about 20 passengers, to Ayers Rock, some 200 miles away. The pilot walked up the aisle of the plane with a cup of coffee on a saucer, sat down in the cockpit, and off we went. After takeoff, he opened the cockpit door, and there in the co-pilot's seat was only his cup of coffee and no co-pilot. He needed that coffee, because he flew that plane like a fighter pilot. In the hot thermal air, it made for a bumpy ride, like a roller coaster. We arrived at the airstrip near the Rock safely. Took a taxi to our motel, and tucked in for the night.

The next day we climbed the Rock. It's a huge red rock over 1000 feet high in the middle of nowhere. It is a spiritual symbol that the aborigines have worshipped for years. To get to the top requires about a 2 hour climb. In the beginning, where it is the steepest, there is a chain rope to hang on to. Thank goodness! After much huffing and puffing we reach the top.

The view is grand. Miles and miles of scrub bush and red earth. Twenty miles to the west is a lumpy rock formation call the Olgas. We rest for a while, and then climb down. That sounds easier than it was. It's still quite steep. Later at sunset, we all gather at a viewpoint called "Sunset Strip" a few miles away to watch the spectacular colors on the Rock.

Wow! What a sight.

We packed up our stuff the next day, and flew back to Alice Springs. Now, with no train tickets available, we have to take the BUS to Port Augusta which is an 850 mile, 30 hour bus ride, with only a few stops, no food, nothing to see, and lots of bumpita-bumpita. The road started out as a proper highway, but soon turned into a rough and very dusty gravel track. One of our stops was Coober Pedy, an opal mining town, much of it underground, due to the intense heat of the desert. At this stop, a couple of opal miners got on the bus. After a few beers they began flashing vials of raw opals for sale. We bought three small opals for $12. What a bargain that was! Well, maybe it was my mini-skirt.

That bus ride was the worst ever. The air conditioning broke, (with the temperature near 100,) and there was only one other female on board, a bunch of half shined miners, and a few scallywags. I was very happy to get back to a hard surfaced road again. By now I need 29 beers.

Ladies of the Rail

I have been in South Africa for a couple of weeks with my husband and daughter. We are driving our hire car and headed to an area called the Karoo. It is a flatland with large farms. We stop for lunches on the way in a small town …go to a milk bar and get some "takeaways." We get three Stewart hot meat pies, crisps (potato chips), soda and apples. Then we eat our lunch at a picnic area along the roadside.

The railway line between Kimberley and DeAar is straight as an arrow and the trains here run flat out with whistles blowing at all the crossings. Now many of the steam locomotives that run this section have ladies names. The names are displayed on plates mounted on the front of the smoke box in gold letters in honor of the driver's wives or girlfriends. There are names like Sharon, Jennifer, Susie, Katie, Sally, Lindy-Lou, Maria and many more. These "Locomotive Ladies" are all lovingly maintained, with the brass on them spit-polished and gleaming. They are painted black with red wheels and white rims on the driving wheels. They are a sight to behold!

My husband Bob stops the car at the signal cabin to check the times of the Ladies running on the rail today. It is a double track here, so we could get trains in both directions to photograph. He returns and says "Amanda is coming through soon, so we will chase her. There is a rough gravel road which parallels the tracks and allows us to get several shots at different spots and even to pace her at the same speed. Let's go get set up to take some fine photos." We find a nice spot near the track and set up. Look, I see smoke! Amanda is coming and she is going like the clappers. What a sight! There is little wind so the smoke trail is laying right over her.

Got a nice shot – now hop in the car quickly and go like a bat-out–of-hell to the next spot.

We are driving on gravel which is rather slippery but we must catch her and pass her by quite a margin in order to photograph her again. We are crazy with excitement! When we catch up to her, the clatter she is making is deafening. She is going so fast, it's a bit blurry. Well, we are going super-fast too, all the while taking movies and snapshots through an open window. We take turns steering, so Bob can shoot too. Sixty miles per hour on gravel, hoping no donkey carts are on the road. Faster we go to find the next spot. Now we're about 30 seconds in front of her. Oh! There's a perfect spot, but we're going too fast to stop there. Maybe we'll go a little further.

We see our spot. Brakes full on to stop and then slam the car into reverse and full speed backwards to get the car in the right position. Again brake hard, slipping and sliding - then suddenly the car does a sharp right turn into a small embankment. BAM!!! We hit it hard, just in time for Amanda to charge on by with the crew hanging out of the cab window laughing and waving at us.

Now, we survey the inside the car. Our daughter is on the floor in the back seat with wide eyes. The tripod, which flew like a projectile from the back seat, managed to luckily miss all of us. Bob checks the car outside to look for dents and bangs – don't want to have to go to the panel beaters before we turn it in.

What a wild ride we had, but by now we are all laughing. Let's drink a soda, eat some crisps, and wait for the next Lady of the Rail to charge by. Maybe it will be Katie, Maria, or Lindy-Lou.

Vive la France

The year is 1970. Bob and I were still in emotional trauma after losing our son. Our dear friend Bill was flying to Paris. He was going there for his job to the Paris Air Show and his wife Mary Jane was going with him for a vacation. They begged us to come to France with to them. We were both excited to do this as it was our first overseas trip.

With passports and suitcases in hand we boarded our plane, a Pan Am 707 to Paris. The movie for that trip was "Lost in Space." Well, that did not give me a secure feeling. Our friends meet us when we arrive at DeGaulle airport, and we go to our hotel. It is located by the Opera House. We get in this open cage-like elevator and go to the fifth floor. Our views out the windows are the rooftops of the surrounding buildings with pigeon feathers and poop everywhere. I can't believe I'm actually in Paris! My French heritage is here and this place is also the fashion capitol of the world.

We went with our friends to dinner at a small sidewalk café. I am wearing a white top, long purple vest and matching miniskirt that I had made. As I look around at the Parisian ladies around me I realize that my miniskirt it is too long, so I roll it up at the waist. Wow, it was now a bit drafty! The glitter of the Champs-Elysees, the hustle and bustle of the city, the shops, the lights, the outdoor cafes, all were enchanting. The girls riding their small motor bicycles draw me in like a magnet. I like those. My favorite was a Solex bike that you pedal first, and then push the small motor lever down to engage it by friction to the front wheel. And off you go. I want one!

We must go up the Eiffel tower, so we get up early the next day to avoid the long lines. The view from the top is stupendous. Before we go down, we use the toilet. Bob goes in the men's door. I go in the women's door. And guess what?! There we are inside looking at each other, because we now have to pay the same person 5 Centimes each (2 cents). We both get a sneak peek of the other side. Vive la France!

The next day, Bob goes to get the rental car and his first big challenge is the huge traffic circle around the Arc de Triomphe. My challenge was to go to the Galleries Lafayette, about five blocks away. I want to buy a sexy black lace bra. With a lot of hand signals and giggling, I find the one I want, pay with my Francs and find my way back to the hotel. This may put some spark back in our lives!

We see the other sights of Paris, say goodbye to our friends, and are off in our rental car to the French countryside. We stop in a small town to buy petrol. The town had a bad storm and the power was out. The man sold us our petrol out of a can and wrote our bill in the dust on the trunk of the car with his fingers. Laughing and nodding, we pay and are off again.

It's lunch time now and we stop at a local café. There are lots of cars here, so the food must be good. The waiter set us at a table for two, in the middle of the crowded room. Everyone but us is busy chatting in French. We just want a simple and quick ham & cheese sandwich, but the menu is all in French, with big, fancy named food on it. So with a few French words like Jambon and Frommage, we order our sandwich and drinks. We wait, and wait, and …wait.

Then finally, our order arrives. It was a whole loaf of French bread, about 4 inches high, 10 inches long, sliced horizontally with pieces of ham and cheese hanging out. Well, I took one look at that and had no idea how I could eat it, so I got the giggles. I could not stop laughing. Bob starts kicking me under the table, muttering "Shut up damn it" under her breath.

Well the more he did that, the more I laughed. We are now the focal point of the café. So Bob carefully wraps this monster sandwich in a napkin, pays our bill and we leave. I am so weak from laughing; I can hardly walk to the car. We manage to eat this monster like cave men, in the privacy of our car.

When we got home from our trip, Bob bought me a Solex motor bike. Riding around the neighborhood, I imagine that I am now that French girl in Paris on her motorbike.

Vive la France!

Rabbit Ears

Now we all know that real rabbits have ears. That's one kind. The second kind is the old fashioned TV antennas that we called rabbit ears. This story is about the third kind, Rabbit Ears Pass in the Rocky Mountains which is 50 miles northwest of Denver on Highway 40.

The year is 1960. We were planning a trip to California and Nevada, but were having a lot of car problems with our '55 Ford. Both doors were sprung and there park gear was broken. So you always had to park on level ground or use the emergency brake. Our friend offered to trade cars with us for our trip. We said "HELL YES" because he had a '57 Corvette! So westward we went in his car. This was our first time, so I packed all summer clothes even though it was November. California would be warm, right?

A couple days of good travel and we are in the Motel 6 in Golden, Colorado. Golden is a suburb of Denver and the home of Coors beer. The motel was across the street from the brewery. The air was gloriously pungent with the soothing smell of fresh beer. YUM!

The weather has been cool, but nice. As I look to the west, the Rocky Mountains rise so majestically. There is a big gray cloud over them, but not to worry because California is just on the other side. It will be warm when we get there, right?

The drive on US40 out of town is good. First we go over Berthoud Pass at 11000 feet. Rabbit Ears Pass is only 9000 feet, so it should be a piece of cake. As we ascend up Rabbit Ears Pass, the clouds start to look ugly. We keep driving anyway. A few snowflakes start falling, then more. Pretty soon there is about 4 inches of snow on the ground and the road is a bit slushy. This road is very narrow and only has two lanes. A few miles later, we are in a full blown blizzard. We want to turn around but visibility is so bad and there are NO guard rails.

All of a sudden out of the snow comes a snow plow blasting down the pass headed right at us. OH MY GOD, he is going to hit us! Bob slows down the car, then brakes but the road is so steep and slippery. The brakes are on, but we are still moving. We are sliding down the road, sideways now. With no guard rails, soon the car starts sliding down the mountainside. Holy crap! Bob yells "GET OUT!" We fall out of the car and land in the snow. The snowplow passes us and continues to plow its way down the mountain.

We watch the car slowly slide down the mountainside. It goes down about 100 feet, then stops. A small bush has kept it from going to the bottom. Bob crawls down to the car, and turns the engine off, grabs my purse and crawls back up to me.

Here we sit in snow with only summer clothes on, shivering. We crawl up to the road, stand up, and wait for a car to come. After about 20 minutes, someone finally stops and offers to take us down the mountain to a gas station in the small town of Kremmling. Joe, the guy at the gas station, sold us chains for the tires and invited us to his home for lunch. After lunch, Joe put on his long underwear and heavy coat; because he said he would be up on Rabbit Ears Pass for the rest of the day pulling cars back on the road. So off we three go in his tow truck back up the mountain.

Joe hooked our car and pulled it up to the road. We put tire chains on, paid him, thanked him and hugged him. We were on our way again. It was still snowing like hell, but the road had been plowed and we had CHAINS. So we pulled into Steamboat Springs that night thankful to be alive. We both said "Let's go South" to a better route. We also took the opportunity to buy some more layers of clothes to wear before we got to California.

Money and Moonlight

It's a warm sunny day in beautiful Bulawayo, Rhodesia. The streets are lined with large Jacaranda Trees and they are in full bloom. The blossoms are a delicate shade of purple and the air is filled with their sweet fragrance. Bob and I are driving our hired car, looking for a bank. There it is, so we park the car and walk in. We are cashing some traveler's checks, exchanging them for local money. We also asked them if they have any new shiny Rhodesian coins for this year, 1974. It's a hobby of ours to collect coins from our world travels. The teller says that the manager of this bank is also a coin collector, and went to get him. His name was Piet and he was quite interested to talk to us lone Americans. Piet was a tall, broad shouldered man dressed in a beige suit, sporting a mustache and a large smile. We talked for a few minutes and then he invited us to his home for lunch. Little did we know what a great friendship this would be over the years to come?

His home, a brick ranch with a fence all around. At the gate, we were met by the family dog, a large German shepherd named Major. In the house we met Alice, his wife, and Louis, one of their four sons. Alice was very friendly and had prepared us a nice lunch. We ate outside on the veranda, had a great talk, and exchanged American coins for Rhodesian coins. Piet was especially excited to get some U.S. Kennedy half dollars.

After lunch we headed north to Victoria Falls, some 200 miles away. The two lane road had very little traffic, only a few cars along the way. At Victoria Falls, we stayed at a quaint cabin in a nearby town. The next day we drive out to the falls, one of the Seventh Wonders of the World. How beautiful! Victoria Falls is on the Zambesi River, the border between Rhodesia and Zambia. At all the viewpoints, there are no guard rails. It's about a 300 foot drop to the bottom, so make sure you always stand by someone you trust.

Later, we inquire at the plush Victoria Falls Hotel if there are any other special attractions to see. We sign up for a side trip after dark to a native camp for a braii (a barbeque) and entertainment. When we arrive, we see there is no electricity here. The camp is illuminated only by a large bonfire and Tiki torches placed around. On the dinner table, there was ordinary food plus "mealies," the native staple of corn meal mush. It looks like paste, tastes like paste, and you could probably use it for paste.

After the braii, there was entertainment. This included some dancing by men and women of the Shangaan tribe in their full native costume. The most impressive act was a young Shangaan man who picked up a six foot length of railroad rail with only his teeth. He had a leather strap around the middle of the rail, which formed into a mouthpiece that he put in his mouth, and never using his hands to pick the rail up. Wow! Afterwards, we bought a few carved masks, then hopped back on the bus to town.

The next day, we were on the road again to Wankie Game Park. Along the roadside, kids were hawking fresh oranges, and sometimes handmade animal figures. Finally we turn into the entrance to the Park. Wankie is a huge game reserve covering several million acres, mostly without fences. We check in at the main camp. Main camp is a cluster of rondavels (native huts) with a fence around them to protect the humans. We rent one of these rondavels for our overnight stay. You can drive throughout the park by day viewing the animals from your own car. But at dusk, all the visitors have to be back in camp, for their own safety.

Tonight we are lucky because once a month around the full moon, there is a special viewing at Nyamandhlovu Pan, a popular watering hole for the animals. We arrive there, walk up the steps to the viewing platform, and quietly wait. All animals come for a drink before they go to sleep, but not all at once. They come and go with their own kind in an orderly fashion. Some even came in line, like soldiers.

First come the cheetahs, then the giraffes, next the elephants. The elephants enter 50 or more from the left, then 50 or more from the right. Mamas and babies are first, then the bulls. Mongoose and guinea fowl arrive also, coming in line. After they have their drink and leave, we hear, then see hundreds of Cape buffalo coming. They are not as orderly as the other groups. Some skirmishes even take place. The buffalo were the last of the big groups to come. What a sight! I am sure the ritual goes on every night.

This moonlight spectacular is now forever etched in our memory.

Just a Little Pot

We fly from New Delhi, India to Lahore, Pakistan for a week in 1979. Through the grapevine we have heard of a hotel in Lahore called "Falettis," so we book a few days there. It was a very nice place with an attached dining room. We ate dinner there two nights, and had very good Western food. On the third night, we got really brave and ordered a local specialty called Korma Kabobs. Holy cow! That was the spiciest and hottest food ever. After five Coca-Colas, our mouths were still burning. I was afraid to pass gas, or I might start a fire.

The culture here is quite different. It is a Muslim country and a man's world. The men here wear loose shirts and very large baggy pants. When you see a woman in public, (not often,) she is wearing a Burka. It is black, and it's like a tent on your head, floor length, with an oval screen over the eyes to see out. I'm a fish out of water here. The men are all leering at me. I feel so exposed, like I'm naked. I grab Bob's hand with a death grip. It's really quite scary.

On Thursday we board a train for Peshawar, at the foot of the historic Kyber pass. The passenger cars are segregated. Men in one, and women and children in another. It is a 12 hour train ride. It was comforting to be with a bunch of women, but frightening to be alone. I was lucky that I sat by some young gals who spoke perfect English, and loved to talk about movie stars.

Time flew by. Bob, not so lucky. He was in a carload of men only. They smoked, chewed tobacco, and spit on the floor. For a change from this, he occasionally ran up to the engine driver, and begged a cab ride. Lucky for him.

We arrive in Peshawar near midnight and the only thing left in the taxi line were three donkey carts, so we hire one. Bouncing along on the back of this donkey cart, I am tired and want to quit. The first hotel we check is full up, and we trot off to another one. They do have a room for us. We also talk to the desk clerk, to arrange for a taxi driver for tomorrow to chase the Friday-only train up the zig-zags of the Kyber Pass to Landi Kotal at the top. The Pass is on the border between Pakistan and Afghanistan. Even back then, it was a rather tense and dangerous place.

Bright and early Friday morning (also our wedding anniversary,) a taxi driver meets us at the front desk and we are off to chase the train. This steam train is special. It has an engine at both ends of the train to go up the steep grade in a zig-zag fashion. The day is sunny, and the sky is clear. The road we are on parallels the track most of the way. The small villages along the way are all fortified. This is the land of the guns, and guns rule. We have a good chase with lots of photographs. At Landi Kotal, the summit, all males from 10 to 100 are walking around with AK47s. I'm trying to feel small in this taxi. Our driver gets us a bite to eat, and we leave town following the return train. A week after we are in the Kyber Pass, the Russians came to Afghanistan, and they closed the border for years.

We stayed overnight in Peshawar, and the next morning our driver takes us to a local bazaar. I need to shop! This bazaar was on a main street with colorful items of all kind for sale. I spied this copper teapot and just had to have it. After the price bantering, I have my teapot, and we begin our long taxi ride back to Lahore to catch a plane to India. In Lahore, we say good-bye to our kind taxi driver.

At the airport customs, they ask us if we have purchased anything while in Pakistan. I say "We just bought a little pot." In an instant, there was a tall, cocky policeman demanding I open my suitcase. So I unzipped it on the airport floor, and he started throwing my clothes, pants, bras, underwear, dresses, everywhere. I was horrified! There, at the bottom of the suitcase, in a brown paper bag was my teapot. When he saw what it was, he was so pissed off; he stood up, clicked his heels, and stomped off. We still laugh at this story.

Surround yourself with people who make you hungry for life, touch your heart, and nourish your soul.

Unknown

Debbie Shew

New Beginnings

BIOGRAPHY

First time writer Deborah Shew was born in Pontiac, Michigan. She moved to Clinton, Montana in 1978. Several years later she returned to Michigan to be with her family. Deborah resides in the area with her husband Larry.

The following is an excerpt from a romance novel that Debbie is working on.

In the completed piece of fiction, a woman with a broken heart finds love and intrigue in Montana. Enjoy the first two chapters.

CHAPTER 1

Jillian sat on the steps of her apartment building watching the moving men take the last of what was left of the life she had shared with George. She had donated all their furniture to St. Peter's Women's Shelter and the rest of her belongings had been shipped to the States. She had it shipped to her best friend, Martha, until she arrived there next week.

After the men had gone, she went upstairs for one last look around. As she went from room to room, she was suddenly hit with all the terrible memories and instantly she was back to that fateful day and she remembered it all step by step.

Jillian had unlocked the door with her key, entered the foyer and threw her keys into the little antique dish that she and George had bought on one of their adventures.

"George, "she shouted. "Are you here?"

No answer. She walked into the den and he was not there. Today was the day he was supposed to be back from the hiking trip he had gone on with his friend, Peter. *Maybe they got delayed, she thought.* Changing into a pair of jeans and a tee shirt, she went into the kitchen to pour herself a glass of wine when she heard the front door buzzer.

"Hey, handsome, forget your keys again?"

"Uh, Ms. Barnes, my name is Inspector Stewart."

"Oh, sorry, "said Jillian. "I thought you were my fiancé."

"May I come up?" asked the Inspector.

"Is something wrong?"

"Yes, there is."

Jillian's heart was pounding.

"Please show your ID to John at the front desk."

Five minutes later, she heard the knock at the door. Her hands were shaking as she opened the door.

"Ms. Barnes?"

"Yes, Inspector, please come in."

She led him into the living room and offered him a seat.

"What's this about?" she asked.

The Inspector cleared his throat, "Two days ago, a man reported that he and his friend were hiking and his friend lost his footing and fell over the edge of the cliff.

Jillian could feel the blood draining from her face.

"My fiancé and his friend were due back today from a week long hiking trip."

The words kept going through her head. *Please let it be Peter. Please let it be Peter.* Suddenly she felt the room spinning around and she could hear carnival-like music, it was like she was in a game show. And the winner is … George Mansfield!

"Wake up, Jillian. Please wake up."

Jillian could hear the words, but she couldn't open her eyes. She struggled to open them and then finally she saw her Aunt Sylvia standing over her.

"Oh, thank God," she said.

There was a man standing next to her Aunt.

"Glad you could join us, "said the man. "My name is Dr. Warner.

"What happened?" asked Jillian, still sounding groggy." You passed out in your apartment and fell.

"Where's George?"

Sylvia was holding Jillian's hand.

"You've been in a coma for a week, "said Sylvia. "When the hospital called me, I caught the first plane to Paris."

Jillian closed her eyes. She remembered waiting for George to come home. He was late. She looked at her Aunt, "I remember talking to a man."

Sylvia left the room. When she reached the hallway, she saw Inspector Stewart coming down the hall towards Jillian's room.

"Does she remember anything yet?"

"No, only that she was waiting for George and that he was late."

CHAPTER 2

Jillian tossed and turned until finally at 6am, she decided to get up and make some coffee. She was sitting at the counter in the kitchen when Scott came in.

"Wow, you're up early," he said.

"Sorry, I hope I didn't wake you but I couldn't sleep."

"No, I was awake, I could smell the coffee brewing. Rachael always got up before me and made the coffee. Did Annabelle sleep through the night for you?"

"No, she woke up around 3 a.m. I fed her and she went back to sleep."

Scott picked up the square device that was sitting on the counter.

"It's a baby monitor," said Jillian. "I like to have it with me so I can hear her when she wakes. Here, look. You can see her in her crib."

As she poured the water and stirred the oatmeal the baby cooing made her smile. *What a sweet sound.*

Scott that close to her in the kitchen stirred a feeling that had been dormant in her for a long time. He was extremely handsome. Tall with brown hair, light stubble of a beard perfectly trimmed, and he dressed very GQ. When he interviewed Jillian he was wearing a pair of worn jeans, no shoes and a white tee shirt.

They enjoyed the hearty breakfast of eggs, bacon and homemade blueberry scones a recipe Jillian had gotten from her mother. Annabelle's breakfast consisted of mashed bananas and cereal. She squealed when she saw her daddy and displayed a toothless grin.

"I'm going to the office to work for a few hours," said Scott.

"Will you be home for dinner?" asked Jillian.

"No, I 'm meeting with clients for dinner and drinks. What are your plans?"

"I thought I would take Annabelle to the park. It's such a beautiful day."

"Sounds like fun." He leaned over to give Annabelle a kiss.

Jillian could smell his cologne. Armani. She was sure of it. *I'm so lucky to have gotten this job*, as she reached over to wipe drool from Annabelle's chin. *What a nice family*.

The sun was shining through the thick clouds. Flowers pushed their way up through the ground displaying beauty and fragrance after their winter's nap.

The man across the street was taking out the trash when he lifted his head as Jillian walked towards him.

"Good Morning," he said putting the lid on the trash can.

Before she could respond, he was already walking back to his house. The man next door was backing out of his drive, probably going to work. He waved and drove off. Jillian wondered how much the neighbors knew. *Did Scott tell them that he had hired a nanny to take care of Annabelle?*

Jillian had packed a lunch for the two of them and found a nice grassy spot where she spread out the red blanket. She had brought an easy read romance novel along in case the baby decided to take a nap after lunch.

"Boy, it's hot out today."

Startled, Jillian turned around and saw a young girl standing directly in front of her. She put her hand up to block the sun so she could see.

"Hi, my name's Megan."

"Nice to meet you. I'm Jillian".

"Are you her mother or the nanny?" asked Megan.

"I'm her Nanny."

"Most of the women here are the nannies," said the young girl. "Their rich mother's hire us so they can go and spend the day shopping or whatever if you know what I mean." Megan laughed apparently realizing that Jillian did not. "Are you a live – in?" asked Megan.

"Yes." Jillian was getting annoyed with all the questions.

"I'm a live-in, too. Toby, the kid I take care of is a brat but it's an okay job for now. His dad is always hitting on me. He told me that if I didn't go to bed with him he would tell his wife that I was making advances. I needed a job and a place to live."

Jillian couldn't believe what she was hearing. Megan couldn't have been more than 20 years old. The conversation was getting on Jillian's nerves. She got up and started putting her stuff in the diaper bag. "It's time for her nap."

"Sorry if I offended you," said Megan. "I have a bad habit of coming right to the point. I think that's why my dad kicked me out of the house. He told me I had a sharp tongue."

When Jillian returned home she put Annabelle down for her nap. She went into the kitchen to make a pot of tea. Waiting for the water to boil, she sat down at the counter to check her cell phone. Two messages and one saved message. She went to her voice mail.

Hi Jillian, it's Max. Just wanted to know if you were still coming this weekend? Give me a call. The next caller was Martha Jillian's best friend. *Hi Jill, it's Martha. I'm going to be in Missoula this weekend and I thought we could get together for dinner, give me a call, gotta run, love you bye.*

The next message had been saved on her phone for 3 years. *Hi babe. Just wanted to tell you I love you and I'll see you in a few days.* The last message George had sent her before he died.

The whistling of the tea kettle startled her. She poured the hot water over the peach flavored tea bag in the cup. The aroma made her inhale deeply before taking a sip. It was almost 5 o'clock. She had made a salad for herself and mashed potatoes, peas and applesauce for Annabelle.

Jillian never went into detail about her life in Europe. She told Scott about her family and how they were killed but the rest she kept to herself.

After dinner Jillian got the baby ready for bed and put her down for the night. She looked at the clock. 7pm. And picked up her cell phone to call Max.

"Hello," came a deep voice from the other end.

"Hey Max, I just wanted to let you know I will be there on Thursday if that's ok?

She heard the phone pull away from his mouth. "Hey Ingrid, she's coming home on Thursday. Oh Jill, everyone is so excited to see you, they can hardly contain themselves. Ingrid has been cooking like a crazy woman for the past 2 days making sure she has all your favorites."

"As long as she has Shepard's pie on that list I'll be happy! How's Aunt Sylvia?" she asked.

"She's in the barn right now checking over the new horse she just bought. Hank brought him over this afternoon and she's been in the barn ever since he got here."

Sylvia loved her horses and she had passed that love down to Jillian. After a brief conversation with Max she said goodbye and told him that she loved him.

"You drive careful," and he hung up.

Scott came through the front door. Startled, she jumped. "What time is it?"

Jillian had fallen asleep on the couch reading her romance novel. He hung his coat over the dining room chair and went into wake her.

He looked at his watch. "A little after ten."

She sat up on the couch. "I must of fallen asleep reading."

Scott looked at the book. A romance novel. I didn't take you for a romantic."

"I can be," she put the book down.

"Glass of wine?" asked Scott.

"Sure."

"Red or White?"

"Whatever you have is fine with me."

Scott went into the kitchen and returned with two tumblers of red wine.

"How was your dinner?" asked Jillian.

"Kissing up to clients isn't my cup of tea but it must have worked because I got the account." Scott owned his own marketing firm and he did very well.

He sounded down.

"Is everything ok?" she asked hesitantly.

He looked at Jillian with tears in his eyes. "Tomorrow would have been Rachael's and mine fifth year anniversary."

"I'm sorry," said Jillian.

"It's ok," he said. "I feel guilty for asking her to wait to have children. I wanted to make sure the firm was stable and she had just opened her practice up. The older Annabelle gets the harder it is. Rachael wanted kids as long as I can remember. She would have been a good mom and I..." his voice trailed off.

She looked at Scott with a heavy heart.   They sat in silence.

"I think it's time for me to head off to bed," she broke the quiet.

"Yeah, me too," said Scott."

After goodnights, each went off to their rooms.

"Good Morning," said Scott as he walked into the kitchen. Jillian was flipping pancakes on the griddle. "My god, those pancakes smell good."

"A special recipe," she said as she set a plate down in front of him along with a glass of orange juice and a cup of coffee.

"You're going to spoil me," he said.

Jillian reminded Scott that she would be leaving early Thursday morning for Missoula.

"Yeah, I talked to Carol and everything is set." Turning back to his breakfast, "Jillian, what is in these pancakes? I can't stop eating them."

"Do you promise not to tell?"

He made a gesture of crossing his heart. "I promise, I will take the secret ingredient with me to my grave."

Jillian laughed, "Okay. Its 2 scoops of vanilla ice cream. Instead of milk."

"You're kidding me?"

"Nope. It's my Aunt Sylvia's secret ingredient."

After Scott left for work Jillian put the baby down for her morning nap. Back in the kitchen, she cleaned up and decided to get packed for her trip. Then later, returned Martha's call and told her she would call her when she got to Missoula.

Thursday morning came and Jillian was all ready to go by 8 a.m. Carol showed up promptly at eight. "Have a wonderful time dear and don't worry about anything, we'll be fine."

Jillian said her goodbyes, kissed Annabelle telling her to be a good girl.

How exciting to get to the ranch. It was only 2 hours away. Her gas tank was full and the sun was shining. She stopped to get a coffee at the Brew Station in town. When she opened the door and walked in she could hear the whispers.

"I'll have a large black coffee to go," she told the girl behind the counter.
Reaching into her pocket to get some money to pay, the girl said it already had been taken care of.

"Thank you," she said and headed for the door. She could feel all eyes on her as she walked out the door.

Note: Debbie's finished book is going through the editing process. You will want to buy one to find out what happens.

Debbie Shew Essays

HAPPY FATHER'S DAY

It's a beautiful day today Dad. The sun is shining and you can see the buds on the trees getting ready to open up after their winter's nap.

I hear cars coming down the flag lined drive. There is a breeze blowing and the flags are swaying in the wind as if they were waving to everyone.

Your resting place is quiet. I see people walking the grounds. Some saluting the flags. I see families sitting by their loved one and I wonder, what they are talking about.

I see Mrs. Carter sitting by her son. I have gotten to know some of the family members of the people that rest by you. She sees me and gives me a wave.

This is a beautiful place, Dad. I feel at peace here talking with you. I really miss those phone calls on my birthday when you would call me by my nickname, reminding me that I'm another year older. I would roll my eyes, the same old joke. What I wouldn't give to roll my eyes again!

Mom is doing okay and all the grandkids are good. I wish you could have met the twins and Nicholas's son, Cole. I'm sure you're watching over all of us.

We miss you Dad,

I'll be talking to you.

And by the way... *HAPPY FATHER'S DAY.*

The Christmas Note

Cassandra stood outside on her porch admiring all the brightly lit homes up and down the street, she always looked forward to each Christmas to see what the next new decoration of the season would be. Christmas was her favorite time of year. She enjoyed the hustle & bustle of the season but most of all she enjoyed her family and grandkids.

As she stood on the porch she wondered how her neighbors would be celebrating. The Murdock's next door would anxiously be waiting for their children to arrive along with their children. Their celebration always started a week before Christmas and continued on until after the New Year.

The Carter's who lived on the other side of Cassandra had one child, Will, and he came home every other Christmas with his New York wife who had told Will and her in-laws not to hold their breath for any grandchildren in the near future. So on Christmas Eve you could see the four of them through the window sitting at the table very quietly enjoying a wonderful meal (Mr. Carter was a fabulous cook!) And on the years that Will and Catherine didn't come home, Cassandra would invite them for dinner, but every year they graciously declined.

Christmas was only a few days away and Cassandra had some last minute shopping to do. She headed off to the world of Wal-Mart. It was a beautiful day, snow was falling gently and as the sun peaked through the clouds it looked like diamonds falling from the sky and landing on the ground. Everything had to be perfect, right down to the smell of sugar cookie candles that would burn throughout her house.

After picking up the last of her items, she finally was satisfied that her Holiday shopping was complete. She headed off to the dreaded check out to wait patiently. Cassandra couldn't help notice a young girl ahead of her. She was buying toys, perhaps for her children or nieces, nephew and what looked like the makings of Christmas dinner. When the cashier had finished tallying up her purchase she was $50 short. With the look of horror on her face, she started picking out items to remove from her bill. At that moment Cassandra remembered the time when she was a single mom with two kids trying to make their Christmas as special as she could.

A feeling of sadness came over her and she knew that she wanted to help but didn't want to embarrass the young girl any further. She leaned forward to get her attention and said that she knew how it was to not have brought enough money. The very same thing had happened more often to her than she wanted to admit. The young girl looked at her, *this is all the money I have*.

Without thinking about it Cassandra handed her $50 so she could purchase the rest of her things. The young girl was grateful. She thanked her wished her a Merry Christmas and said that she would like her name and address so she could repay her kind deed. When Cassandra was done checking out, she noticed the young girl was gone. She knew she would never see that money again but felt good about what she had done.

She was heading towards her car when she heard a voice. I have been waiting for you so I could get your name and address. You have no idea how you helped me, I'm a single mom with 3 kids and without your kindness they would not have a Christmas.
Hesitant to give out her information Cassandra decided to take a chance and see if this young girl would come through. They wished each other a Happy Holiday and they both went on their way.

Two months later a letter arrived in the mail. Cassandra did not recognize the return address. She opened the envelope and inside was a note and a picture of three small children in front of a Christmas tree and a neatly folded $50 dollar bill. The note was short thanking her once again for her kindness.

As Cassandra stood holding the note, picture and the $50 dollar bill a smile came across her face. Christmas really was her favorite time of the year.

Connie Sypniewski

THIS

AND

D

THAT

Connie Sypniewski

Dedication

This Memoir must be dedicated to many people.
First and foremost, to my beloved father who I will miss every minute of every day until I meet up with him again.

To my dear friend, Debbie, who literally dragged me kicking and screaming into the first Creative Writing Class. I'm so happy you were so persistent. Please know I truly value our friendship.

To Susan, the person who truly opened a whole new world for me. I am eternally grateful for your patience and guidance.

Finally, to my husband and my family. Thank you for listening to my ideas and my half written stories. You are my cheerleaders, rooting me on to continue on this fantastic journey. Thank you, thank you!

BIOGRAPHY

In the twilight of her years, Connie Sypniewski has discovered a real love for the written word.

A native of Pennsylvania, she enjoys writing about her childhood, her family and the loving relationship she enjoyed with her father.

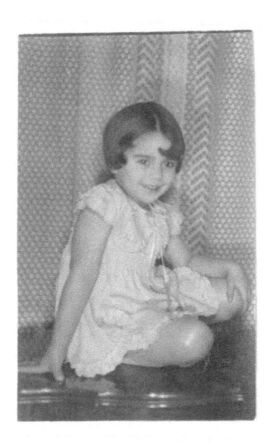

CONTENTS

AWESTRUCK

How do you spend your Thanksgiving holiday? Cooking dinner, going over the river and through the woods to Grandmother's house or -- wait for it -- watching our mighty Lions play their annual Thanksgiving Day game.

Since I am a multi-tasker, I usually cook and watch the game at the same time. Being an organized freak, most of my prep work was already done this year and so I had time to watch at least the first quarter of the game.

My sugar free iced coffee in hand, I settled into "my spot" on the sofa and flipped on the television. Just in time, as the opening bars of the Star Spangled Banner were just starting to be played. A 12 year old African American boy, complete with braces on his front teeth, started to sing. I'm very emotional when it comes to this song, but I was absolutely blown away. The television cameras panned to the players from both teams and they looked awestruck. This child was magnificent. When he finished the song, the crowd went wild and our Lions formed a line and each one shook his hand. My husband and I both wiped the moisture from our eyes and just sat there.

The next day FOX News commented about the performance so I thought I'd try to find out a little more about this young man. He was runner-up in the America's Got Talent Show. I never was able to find out where he was from but his name was Quintaveous Johnson. I went beyond the Google article to read the comments made by other readers.

The first comment was "The name is so amazing its' bearer has no choice but to cultivate a life and personality and style worthy of the name." Another comment, "Best part of the game." Another comment was "Bizarre name. He looks about 20 to me. Once he hits puberty, his voice is gone, unless his parents are doing a Michael Jackson on him." I can't possibly imagine what that may mean. However, someone responded to that comment by saying "You are the only one who said that. No matter what article you post on, you contribute only ugliness and bitterness. Happy Thanksgiving!" My favorite comment was "Reference for the uninformed - switch to the news of the 12 year old black boy who was shot in Cleveland."

My point is that this young man gave a performance that would rival any opera star or any of the other performances by rockers or rappers. Yet there are people out there who hide beyond the anonymity of the internet to spew their bitterness and hatred.

Most of the people were so busy making fun of his name, they didn't have one teeny nice thing to say about the wonderful performance given by a 12 year old boy named Quintaveous Johnson. I am certain we will be hearing much more about this very talented young man.

Beware of Barking Dogs

Is there anyone among us who does not or has not had sore feet at one time or another?

Well, I certainly did and after weeks of painful walking and evenings of soaking my toes, I finally went to see my foot doctor. My great toes were killing me!

I have known this very pleasant doctor since 1993 and he has done several major procedures on both feet such as hammer toes and the ever glamorous bunions. Nevertheless, my feet are extremely sensitive so I am really leery of letting him look at them.

In he saunters and I launch into my routine.

"Are you happy today, Doc?" "You didn't have a fight with your wife or anyone else, did you?"

"Everything's cool," he says laughingly.

No way is he taking his frustration out on my feet, no siree!!

"Okay," I say. "Take a peek and tell me what has to be done with my aching toes, without pain!" "My uncle, Guido, is out in the lobby and if he hears me scream, you're in big trouble!"

"Just do it," I say. "I don't care how much it hurts afterwards; it just can't hurt while you're doing it!"

"I promise that you aren't going to feel a thing!" "My assistant is coming in and we're going to numb you up and we can get started."

"Shots," I say. "In my toes!" "Is this an April fool's joke?" My voice is getting louder and louder and I yell out for his assistant, who is a good friend of mine, and she comes running in with two gigantic syringes.

"Don't worry," she says. "This is the strongest stuff we have."

Is this supposed to make me feel better?

"Go out in the lobby, wake up my husband and tell him to get in here; Doc's going to cut off my great toes!"

In he comes, laughing.

"What's the problem?" he asks.

Could he not see the two big syringes that were going to be stuck into my toes?

We get started and the honest truth was that it hurt...a lot! Let me stick a needle in your toe - five times in each one - and you tell me if it hurts.

By now I'm wringing wet and my heart is racing. I'm told by three people that the worst part is over. I got news for them; it couldn't be much worse.

I'm all numbed up now and we proceed. Doc and Gene are talking and laughing.

"I can't believe what he took out of your toe. You must have been in some major pain," says my darling husband.

Duh, I've been whining about the pain for at least two weeks. I've come to the conclusion you have to be dead before a husband will believe that his wife is hurting or is ill. My tombstone will read "See, I told you I was hurting! "Now do you believe me?"

Ten minutes go by and we're all done. Everyone was telling the truth. After the shots, it absolutely did not hurt.

Doc's assistant gift wraps my toes in Hawaiian Blue tape and all I have to do is soak my tootsies in warm water and put antibiotic salve and a cloth bandaid on three times a day. That won't be a big deal.

Well, that wasn't bad at all! I have the best doctor in the world.

I have to say I was a little disappointed. I at least expected a lollipop or two!

CHILDHOOD - THEN & NOW

Do you ever take some time and sit back and reflect on your childhood? Do you remember how wonderful and uncomplicated it was? While you are pondering this over, what's the very first really clear memory you have? Well, I will tell you mine.

I remember wanting a special baby doll I had seen in a magazine and I was so in love with this doll I tore the picture out of the magazine and carried it with me everywhere I went. This baby doll was beautiful. She had big blue eyes, long eye lashes and red hair that hug to her shoulders in little fat sausage curls. She was full of dimples, on her cheeks, elbows and knees.

Doll babies were different when I was young. The head, arms and leg were flesh colored plastic, but the bodies were cloth, filled with something that looked like white sand. The dolls were always dressed in pretty silky ruffled dresses. They were not skinny hard plastic things.

Oh, how I wanted that baby doll. My mother and father would only look at her picture and smile. Well, Santa Claus brought me that gorgeous doll and I loved her with every fiber of my being. I would say I was about five years old at the time and I spent hours and hours playing with her.

Remember how all the kids in your neighborhood, both boys and girls, would get together and play all day long. We would line up the sidewalks in front of someone's house with chalk and play hopscotch for hours on end. On rainy days, we congregated on someone's front porch and played jacks and marbles. When the weather was good, we all went roller skating.

Skinny Grandma lived just down the alley from us and her street was a dead-end street that ended at the railroad tracks. No one who lived on that street had a car so it became our playground. After dinner, all the kids would congregate in the middle of the street and play. We played simple games like tag, hide and seek, kick the can, dodge ball, red rover and we'd put tin cans on our feet and run up and down the street making noise. There were no fights and there was no bullying. No parent had to get on the phone (if they were lucky to have one) and call around looking for their child or stand on their back porches screaming their child's name. When the street lights came on, you headed straight for home. It was the unwritten law and we all followed it.

During the day, we would play the "let's pretend" games like school and house. Very simple school. Everyone would sit on the bottom steps of the porch and when the "pretend" teacher would ask a question and you answered it correctly, you moved up a step.

We used to play "house" in my friend's Grandma's attic. I had a tea set and an Easy Bake Oven and we scrounged up some old handbags and we were all set to play. I quit playing house when the brother of my best friend pulled me aside and said he wanted to have a D A T E! He spelled it! Damned if I knew what that meant, but I didn't play with him anymore. I ran home and told my Daddy and he just smiled. I think I was about 7 at the time. To this day, I still keep in touch with my first almost date.

Most of us couldn't wait for Saturdays to roll around. We either stayed at home or congregated at one of the houses and listened to the radio. A Date with Judy, Grand Central Station and Let's Pretend. No one made a sound, we were busy hanging on every word that was being spoken.

We all ate with our families and afterwards it was family time. You guessed it, we would listen to the radio. The living room would be dark and

364

creepy on purpose and we would listen to The Shadow, Inner Sanctum with the scary squeaky door, The Green Hornet, The Great Gildersleeve, Jack Benny, Amos and Andy and many more. Every Saturday night, we would hold our breath waiting to hear what would be number one on Your Hit Parade. It was like we were living in a Norman Rockwell Painting, entire families gathered around the radio or the dinner table.

During the summer, when we got older, we would hike down the railroad tracks, swimsuit wrapped in our towels, and head for Camp Tuskareka. The girls would have the even days and the boys the odd. We would spend the afternoon swimming and playing in the water and then head back down those railroad tracks home. No one drove us. We walked.

Now take a look at today and today's children. Most of them have their own cell phones (we didn't have a phone until I was 17 years old, 14-R, and it was a three way party line.) Do you ever see any of them happily playing with about five or six other kids? By playing, I mean the simple fun things where you use your imagination.

Family meals were eaten at home and everyone was at the table. We didn't go to restaurants. Now when you go to a restaurant, no one is talking. Everyone's head is down looking at their cell phones. At the high school, when the bell rings to change classes, there is no talking or laughter. There is no pushing and shoving, all in fun, of course. All the kids have their eyes glued to their phones and are busily texting someone and it's probably the person who was in their last class. Don't misunderstand, I'm not opposed to cell phones for emergency purposes. They can be a lifesaving tool. But shouldn't we be having some human communication with our family and friends?

The games they play are on an I-pad or I-phone or an X-Box. We have two children, a boy and girl, living next door to us. The boy is about

9 and the girl is about 7. I saw them playing outdoors once all last summer. I asked their Dad what they were up to and he said they don't go out much, they play a lot of board games. They are missing their childhood. You can't go out and play hide and seek or red rover when you are 15 or 16 or have a full time job.

Last week-end, my husband and I went to Alexander's for a special dinner. They have wonderful food and the place is usually crowded. As I looked around our immediate area, no one was talking. They were all on their cell phones and only spoke when ordering their meal.

To our left was a very nice looking couple who were texting, maybe each other. For just a moment the lady looked at her dinner partner and smiled. I looked at my husband and said, "Do you suppose he texted her to ask if they were going to have a good roll in the hay when they got home?" Just asking!!

The moral of my rant is to enjoy your family and your childhood. Take time to call your pals on the phone or stop by their houses and invite them outside to play. Turn off the television, the cell phones and the game boxes. Get outdoors and enjoy the fresh air with your friends. Take a walk with them in a rain shower. Build a snowman together. Roast marshmallows on a summer evening. Most importantly, make some awesome memories you won't ever forget!

Childhood is a once in a lifetime chance to have fun and find yourself. It passes so quickly. Take advantage of this fun time. You will have no regrets!

THE EVIL TWIN

I have a sister no one knows about -- she's my evil twin. I try to stay as far away from her as humanly possible, but that is almost impossible.

Somehow she found out my husband was having knee surgery and she decided I couldn't do without her help. She shows up at my doorstep unannounced and, judging from the bags she has packed under her eyes, she's going to stay for a while. God, please give me strength.

She sweeps into my house and I see her x-ray eyes sweep over all of the rooms in my house. You think Superman is good, she puts him to shame. She could teach him a thing or two.

"Oh my, we have lots of work to do before #2 son gets here. Did you just get back from vacation? Do you want your son to think you can't take care of yourself and your home? Assistant living comes to mind. Now let me make a list of what needs to be done," she says.

"The cleaning lady was here two days ago and everything is clean and orderly," I say.

"Well," she snaps back, "certainly not by my standards." "What about the door wall, I see fingerprints."

My God," I think, its 30 degrees out. Does anyone care?

"Our mother always said you were a pig and that you liked living in a mess."

"I'm tired and I'm going to bed. This can all wait until tomorrow."

"That's so like you, always putting off until the last possible moment."

Actually, it's not last minute, we have a day and a half, but I refuse to argue. It's not a battle I would ever win.

I'm off to bed, but really can't sleep. I'm tossing and turning and can't find just the right spot. Suddenly she's standing by my bed.

"Since you can't sleep, why don't you get your fat ass out of bed and throw in a batch of laundry. In that way, you'll be ahead of the game tomorrow."

I swear to the Almighty if had a gun, I would shoot this bitch right between the eyes, chop her up in pieces and put her in the garbage disposal.

Can't do that. So being the obedient one, I stagger out into the laundry room with a basket of dark clothing. I can't fight her so maybe if I do what she says, she'll go away. I can only hope.

"While you're in the kitchen, put those coffee cups in the dishwasher, Never, ever leave dirty dishes in the sink overnight," she says.

Who does she think will be knocking at my door in the wee hours of the morning, the Mayor?

So starts another day. Mind you, she actually has a "To Do" list. I never asked her to stick her nose into my business and I never asked for help. The "To Do" list is very precise. Shower, dress, change sheets on the bed, breakfast, clean kitchen, more laundry (whites this time) after the sheets are done.

It's a beautiful cold sunny winter day, but I am having some difficulty with the sunshine because of cataract surgery. All the blinds in the house are closed and I have dark glasses on. My eyes are burning and watering and I'm miserable.

"It's a beautiful day out, let some sunshine in this house, it's like living in a cave," she says. "And ditch the sunglasses, no Hollywood Scout is looking to sign you up for a part in a movie with George Clooney. You're too damn old."

I patiently explain my problem and her reply is "For Christ's sake, put on your big girl pants and suck it up."

I hate this woman with every fiber of my being.

Back to the "To Do" list, I have to go to the meat store for a few things so off we go. After about an hour of errands, we are back in the the house which is like the Sahara Desert and my eyes are really burning. Does she care, hell no! Gotta keep on keeping on!

"You better wipe the counters in the bathroom so everything is fresh," she says.

I bite my tongue because no one uses the main bathroom and I know it is clean, but I obediently grab the granite cleaner and a cloth and off I go to make it fresh. What's next?? Kitchen, of course. Clean the counters and make sure there's no grease on the stove and vacuum the area rug.

"You just make more work for yourself," she whines.

No kidding! I happen to like the navy blue rug. It matches my kitchen and it gets vacuumed after every meal anyway, so there smart ass!

Almost everything on the list has been completed. Well, I suppose we could paint some walls or pull off some wallpaper.

It's 4 o'clock in the afternoon. She jumps up and tells me that we had better start cooking dinner. After traveling all day, he's going to want to eat and he shouldn't have to wait all night to eat his dinner. My prep work has been done. The potatoes are already peeled and soaking, the salad is made, the asparagus is ready to roast, but it's way too early to start dinner. Okay, anything to keep you happy, you evil bitch.

I putter around the kitchen just so she will think I am busy. Little does she know I'm trying to think of ways to get rid of her? I have some

0.25 mg. Xanax and maybe if I fix her a nice cup of tea and pop four or five of those babies in her cup, she'll sleep and I will be rid of her.

The kitchen door opens and in walks my very handsome #2 son. His father and I are both very happy to see him and we're so comforted by the fact that he is always here when we need him.

The house seems very peaceful. Dinner is cooking, the table is set and the wine is breathing. We sit down for dinner and guess what?? My evil twin sister has gone away. Yeah! I am giddy with joy!

I'll tell you another secret. She will be back tomorrow sitting right beside me throughout the surgery. I just hope and pray that she keeps her big fat mouth shut.

Have you guessed yet?? My evil twin is the other part of me!!

A FATHER'S NIGHTMARE

Everyone's life is different. Some people are happy with what they are and what they have, others continually strive for bigger and better things. Growing up, life is simple. It's fun. There are people taking care of us and they really work hard to make sure we have everything they can give us to make us happy.

We spend a great deal of time wishing our lives away. I wish I was in high school, I wish I was out of college, I wish I could get a better job and the beat goes on. I remember telling my mother that if I wasn't married by the time I was 21, she would find me hanging in the shed. No way was I going to be an "old maid." In this day and age, that would be considered pure insanity.

As the story goes, I married my handsome marine 28 days after my 21st birthday and moved to the State of Michigan. At least I didn't have to kill myself. Just stop and think what my life would have been like growing old in a coal mining town, no handsome rich guys hanging around, only miners and you will probably agree that would be a fate worse than death.

I got married and we had a beautiful family. First two handsome sons and finally a tiny little hairy baby girl. She had hair on her upper arms and on her ears and I can still hear my mother-in-law, "Can't she have a baby that looks like our side of the family?" Nope and I did it on purpose.

My husband was thrilled with our two sons - after all, we all know men think they're not men unless they help produce boys. I vaguely remember that cigars were bought and passed around. We didn't have a lot of extra money so we didn't do a lot of splurging.

Along comes baby girl, all 7 pounds 6 ounces and 19 inches long. Comparing her to the two boys, she was tiny. Well, her Daddy went crazy, he arrived at the hospital with a dozen of beautiful pink roses and a fluffy soft pink blanket. The princess was going home in grand style. Daddy decided she needed her very own blanket and I secretly wondered if he had robbed a bank, but I decided to keep my mouth shut.

And that has always been the story through the years. Don't get me wrong, he unconditionally loved all three children, but he treated her differently. His demeanor on her wedding day was worthy of an Academy Award. He walked her down the aisle with tears rolling down his cheeks. This is a man who truly loves his daughter. The pedestal he put her on is so high, oxygen is required.

So imagine what went on at our house this past Friday. He went off to get a haircut about 1:30 in the afternoon and he's not gone five minutes when the phone rings. Who's calling, our son-in-law, Peter.? I think he has called three whole times in the 35 years they have been married.

He called to tell me that our daughter had checked herself into Emory Hospital Wednesday morning and had been admitted by early afternoon. He flew back to Atlanta from Chicago Wednesday night but waited to call us until Friday so he would have all the information we all needed and he didn't want us to be alarmed or worried. Hah -- he could have had the Pope call and tell us all would be okay and there would still be major alarm in the house.

It took an hour before Gene got back home. He has 20 strands of hair on his head so why did it take an hour?

One look at my face and he knew something was terribly wrong, I told him what I knew. Our daughter was in the hospital in serious condition and had to have emergency surgery the next day, Saturday.

She had an acute case of pancreatitis, her gall bladder was packed with stones, her liver enzymes were through the roof and she had to have surgery immediately. The words cardiac arrest were mentioned.

Gene didn't say a word, just put on his coat and hat and went outside. I watched him walk around the driveway and into the backyard. After about 20 minutes, he came back in and told me I should call the boys and Uncle Tom, which I had already done.

We had a dinner engagement that night at St. Mary's Church and with some reluctance, we decided to go. While there, we could duck into the church and say some prayers. After about an hour and a half, we were headed back home.

As we were leaving the parking lot, the phone rang and it was our daughter asking why we were at church on a Friday night. I told her we were there for the fish fry and prayers and she laughed. She was really upbeat. She wanted to speak with her Dad, but he just shook his head and kept on driving. I didn't have to explain, she said she knew he wouldn't want to talk to her. She told us she loved us and our granddaughter would keep us informed as things happened.

After a sleepless night, it's finally Saturday morning and I refuse to leave the house unless I know something. Finally, around 10 a.m., we learn that the surgery is over and she will be in the recovery room until 11 a.m. Later that afternoon she calls, but her Dad will still not talk with her.

She is now home, recovering and she has finally talked with her Dad several times. All's right with the world. The thing that is eating away at him is the fact that she started being in pain Tuesday evening, for 12 hours, and then Wednesday morning she decided to go to emergency, all by herself. It had to happen that way. Husband is in Chicago, daughter is at work in Atlanta, one son is in Dallas and the other is in Virginia. She said she could have called a friend, but it was too early in the morning. Of course, he feels he should have been there.

Dad is smiling and acting his usual nutty self again. This afternoon, her doorbell will ring, she will go and answer it and the florist will be there to hand her a dozen perfect pink roses with a card that simply says, "I Love You, Dad". He did mention to me that we should have gone out to buy her a fuzzy pink blanket to go along with the roses. And that, my friends, is a very happy ending to something that would have been a disaster. Thank you, God!

THE FIGHTING IRISH!

My dad was a huge football fan. To be more accurate, he was an avid Notre Dame Football fan. He only went as far as the tenth grade, but if he was of this generation, he would most assuredly have been a Notre Dame graduate.

As far back as I can remember, he and I usually spent Saturday afternoons in the front room (as it was called back in the day) listening to Notre Dame football on our RCA radio. (There was no television back then!) My mother would be in the kitchen baking and she would wander in with a plate of fresh baked cookies and glasses of cold milk. Never did she ever interrupt our Saturday games.

So, growing up in that kind of atmosphere, Notre Dame was engraved on my forehead. As I entered adulthood, the engraving on my forehead never tarnished. Instead, it grew brighter.

Neither married life nor motherhood ever changed this love affair. I preached Notre Dame, but my sons had no desire to become part of the Fighting Irish family. I offered free tuition to my grandsons, but they weren't interested.

I watched every game for the 62 years of my marriage. I knew an awful lot about the coaches and players. My wardrobe consists of hats, t-shirts, hoodies and sweatshirts and, as my friends and family will verify, I wear it all.

One of the items on my Bucket List is to visit the campus and take pictures of the Golden Dome and Touchdown Jesus. I want to sit in the stands, I want to walk on the field. It will be a tough trip because so much of my Dad will be there. I am sure he is at every home game cheering on his Fighting Irish.

My grandson, Christopher, is a very loyal Michigan fan and we tease each other about our football teams. At Christmas time, during some of this back and forth banter, I told him that a visit to Notre Dame was on my Bucket List. I looked at him and said, "but if I don't get to visit in person, after I'm gone, I would like you to go to Notre Dame and scatter some of my ashes in front of Touchdown Jesus."

He looked at me, gave me a big hug and he didn't miss a beat. "Sure," he said, "but you know, Grandma, I'll be singing the Michigan Fight Song!"

EPILOGUE

During one of our biweekly telephone calls, my oldest son, Michael, told me he would be coming home for a week's vacation and I needed to block off July 27 - all day - so we could hang out. He wouldn't say any more than that. I quizzed my husband and he said he knew nothing and told me to "just go with the flow!"

So all kinds of ideas popped in my head. I finally decided they were taking me to the Apple Store to get a new I-Mac computer and printer. Okay, that will work!

I had a very restful sleep, and I had a really pleasant dream. My beloved Daddy was standing in the middle of a football field. He was wearing brown trousers and a white shirt and, as usual, the sleeves on his shirt were rolled up. He had the biggest smile on his face; he looked very happy.

Suddenly, I knew! We were going to Notre Dame! When I told my husband, he grinned and said "we just can't put anything over on you! How do you know that's where we're going?"

"Duh, what do you think? My daddy told me." Words can never describe my happiness.

During the two weeks I waited for "the trip," my brain shifted into overdrive. What if I didn't feel well? What if I had a bout of Montezuma's Revenge? Would I embarrass myself because this trip was going to be extremely emotional for me?

Finally, the day arrived and I was very nervous. I felt like throwing up! I had a boulder in my throat and I couldn't get rid of it. This would be a 3 1/2 hour drive and as I watched the mile markers fly by, my anxiety level increased. *Put your big girl pants on, Connie! This is a chance of a lifetime. Don't screw up!*

I had purchased tour tickets on-line and we were scheduled to go on the 1 p.m. tour. We were all set - if I could get a handle on my anxiety. *Come on, girl, you can do this!*

All of a sudden we turned down Douglas Avenue and there it was! The University of Notre Dame, Home of the Fighting Irish! I could see the Golden Dome! It doesn't happen very often, but I was speechless and very teary eyed. I didn't know which way to turn my head. Sure, I expected a lot, but the beauty and serenity of the campus was beyond description.

Notre Dame is a walking campus with wide sidewalks leading up to each building. There are only two roads on which you can drive, but only around the perimeter of the campus. The grass was perfectly manicured, the flowers were in full bloom and tall trees lined the walkways. I saw no weeds or dead flowers and a scrap of paper wouldn't stand a chance. Talk about pristine. Every one of the buildings are made of the same brick and the buildings are huge.

Before our tour started, my son and I went into the basketball arena and it was full of baton twirlers from all over. They were having some kind of event and it looked interesting, but I had somewhere important to be.

Of course, I had to hit the book store that was in the arena. After all, the guide was kind enough to give me a 10% off coupon. I spent most of my social security check there and I was sure that, after I left, they could close up the store because, with what I had spent, they had hit their monetary quota for the day.

Time for the tour to get started. It was 96 degrees and quite humid, but I was determined. Our tour guides told us very interesting facts and great stories about the Gipper and Rudy. Can you imagine what happened next?

I was in the Fighting Irish locker room, little ole me! It was the original locker room built in the 1920's and it was huge and immaculate. If you closed your eyes for a moment, you could almost hear all the players chattering while they were getting dressed for the game. I even ventured into the shower and I could almost smell the perspiration from the players who had just finished playing their hearts out for the Fighting Irish! Next I walked down the stairway, reached up and slapped my hand on the "Play Like a Champion Today" sign and then went through the tunnel to the football field.

The field had been prepared for the upcoming season and it took my breath away. The artificial turf was greener than green with brilliant white yardage stripes. Our tour guides asked us to stay in the end zone and I did just that, even though I had been hell bent on getting to the 50 yard line.

This was a lifelong dream come true and I will tell you that when I stepped in the end zone of that field, I was not only overcome with emotion, but also a sense of inner peace. For just an instant, the sun went behind a small cloud and when it emerged, it seemed a little brighter, at least to me.

I know he was there with me. Thank you, my beloved Daddy, for sharing this special moment with me and thank you for showing me how to love something so much even though it almost becomes an obsession.

When the tour was ended, we walked around and I got photos of the Golden Dome and the Touchdown Jesus wall. On my next trip, I plan on going into the Golden Dome Cathedral and visiting the Grotto. Yes, I plan on going back.

In my next life, I will be enrolled at the University of Notre Dame, Home of the Fighting Irish! My tuition has already been paid!

FOOTBALL

Another year, another football season! From mid-August until the first Sunday in February, football rules Monday and Thursday nights and Sundays from 1 p.m. until midnight. Saturdays are packed with college games. Social engagements are arranged around football games and when the season is over, there is a definite sense of loss. It's like your best pal died.

Girls, for the most part, are not supposed to know or care about football. Believe me, when my children were growing up, we watched football whenever it was on television. I hated pro football Sundays and the only saving grace was the fact that the family was always together. Sunday dinners had to be planned around half time of whichever exciting game everyone wanted to watch.

The years go by in a blink of the eye and we became empty nesters. So what do we do on week-ends, watch football. If we weren't at one of the kids' houses, they were over at our house for dinner and afterwards, it was time for the big game of the week.

My children moved out of state and it was just me and my significant other. What did we do on weekends? You guessed it! Watch football!

I truly took it as long as I could and one sleepless night, I came up with a plan. You know the old saying, if you can't beat them, join them!

So I began to plot and put my plan together. I secretly bought a book at Barnes and Noble called "Football for Dummies" and I installed an AP on my I-phone and I-pad called "Team Stream." I would wake up at 6 a.m. and, while my hubby was making coffee, I would flip on ESPN to watch

Mike & Mike. You have no idea how much information you can get from these two. They critique every game, interview coaches for their opinions and even have players on. I listened intently and I learned. When I didn't understand a position or rule, I would Google it. I made a list of the 32 pro teams and added the names of each quarterback and coach.

Please understand that college ball was always special and exciting for me, but pro ball is a little tougher to comprehend. I was determined to learn so I could join the group at the "big table" and talk with all the Monday morning quarterbacks who had definite opinions about what went wrong and how the outcome could have been different. Men always think they know all there is to know!

Well, times they are a changing! Now I can sit at the table with the worn out would-be athletes and discuss the latest games. I read! I listen! I know stuff! Why would I sit in front of the television all day when I can look up info on Team Stream and listen to Mike & Mike the next day? For example, if they are talking about the New York Jets or the Denver Broncos or whatever team, I listen. Then, when I am with all the would-be players, I can toss out a few interesting tidbits of information they don't know about. I read! I listen! I know stuff!

I can carry on a heated conversation about bad boy Johnny Manziel. You know, they refer to him as Johnny Football. This 23 year old kid is very messed up with drugs and alcohol and his Dad wonders what the NFL is going to do to help him, if anything. Where was the father and mother when he was growing up? Johnny can ponder that burning question when he is standing in the unemployment line. The latest news on Johnny Football is that he is going back to college!

Then there is all the discussion regarding concussions, domestic violence, drug and alcohol abuse and, of course, last year's deflategate. I have an opinion about it, especially deflategate. Tommy didn't do anything - why would he - he's awesome without cheating. Besides, I'm trying to get him over to cut my lawn so I can watch him and drool from my deck. By the way, if you are going to have Tommy over for dinner, you need to know that he does not eat nightshade veggies. That would be mushrooms, peppers and tomatoes and his favorite food is ice cream. See, I told you: I read! I listen! I know stuff!

At first my family, husband and two sons, thought I was hysterical. I let them know that I didn't approve of all the tats, but I have a deep appreciation for the 6 pack abs and the tight butts, and they all agreed that I needed some major help. But time marches on and once in a while I would throw out some information they didn't think I should know. After all, I'm a girl! I know when a quarterback is a pocket passer or is described as having happy feet, I know what an on-side kick is, I know when the quarterback gets sacked (don't you hate it when the bully who did the sacking celebrates) and I know what a long snapper is and the list goes on. Now I am the football guru of the family. My two sons will call me before the game to hear what I think and Dad gets a little out of sorts. He wonders why they are calling me. After all, girls are not supposed to know about football! He gets the phone calls after the games because he sits and watches every play. Me, I read all about it! Come on, say it, I need help! You are probably right, but where is it written that a girl can't like and be knowledgeable about the game of football, man's favorite sport, next to sex, of course.

Today is Super Bowl Sunday and the game is about to begin. I'm ready. There will be yelling and screaming and probably some jumping up and down. Let's not forget cussing. That will happen during the first part of the first quarter and then I'm off to my bedroom. The secret is to wait until my hubby is engrossed in the game and that takes 5 minutes, and then disappear. I have to read some stuff about the game. He never notices and I make sure I'm back in the room for half time.

So, are you ready for some football??

HOLIDAY FUN

'Twas the week before Christmas and all through the Colley household was the sound of raucous laughter.

We believe in punishing ourselves for past transgressions, so we get together an entire week early to laugh, talk and make each other miserable.

The three grandchildren are all grown now with lives and opinions of their own, so the activity has cut down quite a bit.

Grandpa Gene and I arrive first because I am on cookie baking detail and so I expect to be busy for the next several days.

The weather is not very cheerful, haven't seen the sun in four days. Georgia is a bit warmer than Michigan so that will make it a little better.

The three grandchildren (one girl and two boys) who belong to this household are all grown now, the youngest being 26 years of age. We have a Marketing Project Manager, an Infectious Disease Doctor and a Certified Public Accountant at one of the big 8 accounting firms.

No one has ever baby sat these three except Grandma Connie and Grandpa Gene. When they moved from the area, our work vacations were scheduled around babysitting detail. We traveled to New Jersey, Massachusetts, Illinois and Georgia to look after them. We loved playing Lord and Lady of the Manor, but it involved a lot of hard work. But we had so much fun!

These three worshipped the ground we walked on. They hung on every word we uttered. We baked cookies, played games, did homework, went out to dinner and I even taught them how to vacuum the family dog.

As they got older, things began to change. They began to squeal on us, especially Grandma Connie. One time my daughter laughingly told me one of the kids told her I put raisins and grapes in his lunch bag, at the same time. Now I ask you, what's wrong with that?

There is even more change now. They still fall all over us, but they talk back and argue, especially with me. They remind me of all the things I did wrong. Never mind the fact that I traveled from Michigan to wherever they were living at the time to take care of them when their parents were away.

More than fifteen years ago, I made a pineapple upside down cake and used crushed pineapple. Imagine how that turned out. After baking the required time, it seemed a little jiggly and it got poured down the garbage disposal. I heard about this mistake while we were having dessert Christmas Eve.

One day I excitedly asked my granddaughter if she heard the music of the latest teen heartthrob. She looked at me and said, "I'm a little old to be listening to teen age idols and so are you, Gram." I guess I should be listening to a funeral dirge as I work out with all the fine young boys at the gym.

The youngest grandson thinks I should take his dog. He has an important job as a CPA and works a lot of hours and he feels it is not fair to Jackson. Oh, yes, I'm going to take this 75 pound dog who thinks he is a chihuahua home with me. Jackson has a very long tail or should I say whip and he beats the hell out of any one who happens to be close to him. Besides that, he is a non-stop shedder and I would have the vacuum cleaner in my hands several times a day. Dog hair, ugh! I laughed hysterically at the idea of taking Jackson and believe me that will never ever happen.

The child that gives me the most grief is the doctor. We cook and bake together and the teasing banter goes on and if I didn't love him so much, I would strangle him. Wherever I stand, he is standing next to me.

386

Wherever I sit, he is sitting next to me. He has to share me with his younger brother so I get to sit in between these two wonderful human beings. My granddaughter always sits across the table from me. I know she thinks I'm as old as dirt and I think she is watching to see me fall face first into my pasta.

They were all interested in my Christmas article but, when I printed it out, they started to laugh. It seems I had on the same outfit as I did when my photo was taken. "Good grief! We better take Grandma to the mall. She's got the same clothes on!" Grandma, are you poor? Do you need some money?" And on and on it went.

Did I get angry? After all, the focus was on my clothing and not on my article. Maybe, just maybe, I got a little hot under the collar for about a nanosecond, but then I, too, joined in the laughter. These three young people are very comfortable with us and know they can tease us unmercifully.

Later that evening, each one of them came over and gave me a big hug and told me how much they liked the article and how proud they were of me, especially since I'm so old. My age frequently gets tossed into any conversation we may be having.

The evening our doctor was leaving to return to California, he gave me a hug and thanked me for the wonderful cookies and for the good time we had cooking and handed me a CD. Besides being a busy doctor, he found time to compose and play music and I was the one who got the CD. How about that??

Believe me when I say neither Grandpa Gene nor I have to wonder if these three munchkins love us. We are Grandpa and Grandma Cool!

HOLIDAY TIME DOWN SOUTH

It's another warm day in Georgia - Johns Creek, formerly Alpharetta. I should say extremely warm, foggy and rainy. Kind of reminds me of a monsoon, not that I've ever been in one, but I read a lot! The weather has settled down now and the sun is shining brightly.

It's Sunday after Christmas and I decide to venture out on the deck, notebook, pen and coffee cup in hand. Peacefulness wraps its gentle arms around you and you truly feel all is right with the world.

As I am sitting on the deck, I am being entertained by some squirrels running around playing tag. The house overlooks the fourth fairway on a private golf course, Country Club of the South. As I'm sitting here, two sets of golfers drive by and you can hear the whirr of the wheels before you actually see the golf carts.

It is so quiet and peaceful you can hear the conversation among the four golfers. Of course, they are discussing the best methods of hitting the tiny golf ball so it rolls right into the hole. And, of course, each one has a sure fire method of success. They each make their shots and leave the fairway to go onto the next one. No one made it in just one stroke.

As I look across the fairway, there are some pretty big houses. For all the years I have been sitting on this deck, I have never seen a single soul outdoors except for the golfers, lawn people and a few women walking the family pets. In the evening, the houses are lit up so I'm assuming there are human occupants in them.

I'm a little disappointed in the Christmas decorations this year. Usually every house in the subdivision of 700 plus houses is totally lit up. The houses are huge, like mini castles, so you know holiday lighting is farmed out to private companies just as the flower planting is.

There are very few kids around so most of these mini castles are inhabited by two people. Just think, you wouldn't have to see your husband or wife for days if you so choose. Wouldn't that be cool?

Quiet once again falls over me only to be interrupted by two blackbirds having a very loud argument in a nearby tree. They soon fly off and once again it is peaceful.

I am told that it has been so warm for December that some of the plants are starting to bloom and all the grass is still quite green. The leaves are all gone from the trees, but the pine trees, as always, are green and are busily dropping pine needles all over. The needles are not like the ones up north. They are more than twice as long and very sharp. The pine cones that fall are larger, too. Get hit in the head and you may be talking mild concussion.

The pine trees are extremely tall with very skinny trunks. The actual pine part of the tree is way up on top. Sort of reminds me of telephone poles wearing a big fluffy wig on the very top. When it's windy, the entire tree, from the very top to the bottom, sways. If a tree is hit by a tornado, the tree isn't snapped in two. It is completely uprooted.

I am going on and on about the pine trees of the South. On a windy day, it is a fascinating sight to behold. It's like they are doing a graceful dance, sometimes a slow gentle waltz and other times a fox trot or tango. On a really windy day, my husband says they are doing the paso doble, but I just think he likes to say that. Anyway, he doesn't know a tango from a fox trot so he would not qualify as an expert on the subject of swaying trees.

It is very uncomfortable both indoors and out. The air conditioning is on and we have been doing quite a bit of deck sitting. The sweaters I packed are sitting on the closet shelf in hopes of cooler weather. As of today, it doesn't look like that will happen.

So I have come up with a plan. Monday, bright and early, I'll be off to Macy's or Dillards to buy some cooler stuff. Do you think there was a method to my madness?

Shortly after writing this, the weather turned to up North weather. The weather forecasters were predicting snow and ice storms in different parts of the state. The television screen is full of warnings about freezing rain, snow and very icy roads. That's okay, we have the very important bread and milk in the house and it's only the two of us. Another plus for us is that all the electrical wires are underground so we won't have to worry about a power failure. So it's Friday night and we're off to bed. We'll see what happens tomorrow.

Saturday dawns sunny and windy. There are still all kinds of warnings on the television. They are talking about the snowfall and when I look outdoors, there is about a half inch of snow on the car and patio table and that's it. We were warned to stay off the driveway when taking Cooper out because it would be slippery. Take the dog outside from the lower level and just walk out onto the grass. There was no snow on the grass or on the bushes. Interesting, don't you think.

Around 11 a.m., our grandson calls to let us know that he can't come over and spend the day with us because Georgia 400 and Old Alabama are closed. This is getting really funny. Well, it turns out to be a perfect reading day.

At 4 o'clock, we decide to venture out. There are very few cars on the road which is highly unusual. I run into Publix for a few things and the shelves are practically bare. The clerk tells me they had a big shopping surge all day Friday and, as a matter of fact, they are all out of bags, both plastic and paper. Better to come back tomorrow.

These gracious people are hilarious. They are scared to death of snow and ice. I think heavy rainfall also scares them. I can honestly say a true Southerner would not survive a Michigan winter.

HUH?? WHAT??

We all know that famous saying "Old age is not for weaklings." I'll add my very own words to that saying. "Old age requires a hell of a lot of patience." I would also say tolerance, but that means the same as patience.

So I ask one and all, "Why does the aging process take away one's hearing?" Old age is a crucial part of your life. Don't you have to hear what's going on around you so it sinks into your brain and, hopefully, you can respond? Surely you don't want anyone to think you are a deaf mute or think the lights on and no one's home when you give them a blank stare.

Our television has to be played at 55 or 60 so you can't hear the telephone ring. I'm sure our neighbors enjoy the fact they can save money on electricity because they don't have to turn on their television sets. They can listen to ours! Sure hope they are as enamored with Fox News as my household is.

Ask a question or make a statement and the first word you hear is "Huh?" Hearing aids would definitely help, but they have to occupy a spot on the kitchen shelf so they don't get lost. You may want to know why they stay on the shelf. Well, I've been trying to figure that out for about five years now.

We had a very important appointment with the Cardiologist. That means the heart doctor and wouldn't you think that is important? Do we have our hearing aids on? Hell no. The answer I get is, "Oh, I forgot!" Do you not want to know if you'll be alive next month?

Every statement has to be repeated at least three times. Then, human nature being what it is, I feel it necessary to raise my voice.

"Why are you yelling at me?" he asks.

"I'm tired of listening to you mumble when you talk to me."

"How come I can hear my friends?"

"It's you; you have to learn how to speak more clearly."

I'm losing the battle; I'm giving up; it's hopeless.

I have an idea! We should start a new trend. Whenever someone speaks to you, your first word should always be "huh" or "what." After all, if you can't beat them, we may as well join them. Maybe we can start a sign language class at the Senior Center.

"Huh?"

THE INVISIBLE/FORGOTTEN GENERATION

As we grow older and become members of the Senior Brigade, we start to become invisible. The world revolves as if we don't really matter. When is the last time someone outside of your own younger family asked for your advice or opinion? It becomes more difficult to enjoy your life. Of course, I have pet peeves and I'll take it upon myself to speak for my generation.

First of all, there are no sensible shoes. During the warm months, you will find racks and racks of flip flops for both males and females. They are really great for the beach! Put them on the elder set, they look "awesome" on our old fat, swollen feet with the chipped nail polish on our toes, very dry cracked heels and lovely hammer toes. How about the dressy shoes with the 4-inch heels and pointy toes? I am of the opinion you could murder someone with either the heel or toe; one blow directly between the eyes, mission accomplished! Besides that interesting tidbit for your "good to know" file, how in the hell can you walk properly in them? Shuffling down the avenue comes to mind.

So your choice of nice shoes is extremely limited. I have quite a few pairs of New Balance and Ecco shoes in my closet. Expensive, but not fashion savvy. My New Balance shoes will look great with my little black cocktail dress. My plan is to enter a party a few minutes late when everyone is engage in stimulating conversation, find a table and immediately sit down. You do not move from that spot until the party is over and then you're one of the last to leave. Make sure your adult diaper, Depends, is firmly attached. I'm told they work very well and you can sit and enjoy the festivities for hours. No one in the room will ever notice your shoes.

Let's venture over to the dress department. This should be fun and I remain hopeful. You know the saying, the glass is half full. Rummaging through the racks, I quickly become discouraged. Is the entire female population in the 20 to 40 age range? Neck lines cut down to your belly button, hemlines thigh high and colors so gawky you could be working a busy street corner on a Saturday night.

I swear each clothing factory has an evil elf working undercover to further frustrate my generation. A size 10 is marked size 10, but I firmly believe that damn elf changes the tags so that size 10 is really an 8. Is it any wonder you can't get in it?

Next top, fourth floor, Lingerie, Oops! I feel a monstrous headache coming on. First on my list, how about a new bra? I must be delusional. All the pretty bras are one or two hooks when we really need a 3, 4 or 5 hook bra. If a bra has that many hooks, why are they padded? I guess a padded bra with 5 hooks would be great if you were playing lineman for the Green Bay Packers.

Then there are the action sports bras for the athletic female to keep us from jiggling and hurting ourselves. After struggling to get into one, I dare you to look in the mirror. You look deformed! See the resemblance, two little mounds of bread dough under a napkin.

I have a burning question. Do men wear athletic supporters to keep from bouncing up and down or do they even bounce? I have to make it a point to do some research on that. Gee, I wonder if Tom Brady or Adam Levine would agree to be my guinea pig?

Okay it's time for another catastrophe. Panties! All the pretty ones are made for the skinny femme fatales. They hit below the belly button and are cut thigh high, which is supposed to make our legs look longer. Do we really care?

There is no room for a bulge or a wee bit of extra flesh. I dare you to stand naked in front of a full length mirror. Is the Michelin Lady looking back at you? Put on a pair of thigh high bikini panties. I bet you never thought God had a sense of humor. Now I dare you to put on a pair of thong underwear. Who wouldn't get all excited to have a piece of dental floss in the crack of their butt?

Let's face it. We have muffin tops, protruding tummies, sagging breasts, waterfall backs, fat feet, swollen hands and ankles and now our hair and eyebrows are starting to thin. What would you give for a really gorgeous outfit that fits all of your body parts like a glove? I mean no bulges, no dimples or ripples.

Well, all of these smug designers who are making our lives miserable are going to get old and have bulges and ripples someday, and unless they live on a diet of frozen grapes and Dasani water, they will have the same problems we all have. God does have a sense of humor!

Wish I could be a fly on the wall when they go shopping!

JOEY

I am not now nor have I ever been a dog lover. At this stage of my life, I am absolutely certain I will never become one.

Over the years, when all the kids were home, from time to time we would have a dog. Believe me, I only tolerated them.

Fast forward to quite a while after we became "empty nesters." Our daughter decided, on her own with no coaxing from us, that we needed company, something to take care of and enjoy.

"Definitely no dog," I said during many phone calls. Oh she saw the cutest Boston terrier and her husband told her she could rescue it, but couldn't keep it. Enter Mom and Dad.

One early Saturday morning my very favorite grandson called and said, "Gram, we are going to pick up your puppy today!" "What do you want to name him?" Talk about being dumbstruck. How many time have I said we didn't want a dog.

"Gram, did you hear me?" "What should his name be?"

In a split second of insanity, I blurted out, "Joey."

We were assured our daughter was buying the puppy, having him neutered and trained and would happily take care of him while we spent three months in Alabama. To sweeten the pot, she bought a dog crate, a ceramic bowl with his name on it and a travel crate so he would be comfy when we traveled. Did I mention a bag full of doggie toys? How lucky could we be?

We picked up Joey three months later, all trained and obedient and brought him to our home in Michigan. Joey immediately fell in love with

Gene and looked at me with complete indifference. I was the wicked witch of the household.

If I came into the kitchen, he would leave the room even if he was eating. If I put out his food, he looked very confused and had to be coaxed to eat. If his master wasn't home or not feeling well and I had to take him outdoors, he would start to shake the minute I reached for his leash.

I paid him absolutely no attention whatsoever. There was no affection between the two of us. The amazing part was that he was very obedient with me. I gave him his baths and he sat in the tub and didn't move a muscle. He walked on a leash right by my side and if I stopped, he would stop. I have been told by my family that the poor dog feared for his life.

Ours was a hate-hate relationship for almost 14 years. Gene took care of the daily stuff and I took care of the grooming, bathing and health issues. Joey didn't want for anything except my affection. Please understand, as I tried to explain many times to family and friends, I do like dogs. I just never want to own one.

Joey suddenly became very ill and a mass was discovered in his stomach and we had to send him over the Rainbow Bridge to doggie heaven.

I truly miss him! After the fact, I know I missed out on 14 years of unconditional love from a beautiful black and white Boston terrier named Joey.

THE LAST CHAPTER

I have a confession to make. I have a serious illness and I am not doing a very good job of handling the situation. I have kept it a secret for about a year now, but each day I get a little worse.

My illness is very serious to me. It keeps me awake wondering what I can possibly do to avoid the inevitable. I lay awake at night and ask myself how long will it be before family and friends start to notice and start with the pity parties thrown in my honor.

Try as I might, I will not win this battle so eventually this illness will put me in my grave. What's wrong with this lovely little lady with the dancing brown eyes and the smile as big as all outdoors? Everyone knows I'm a control freak, but I seem to have no control over this.

Before you all flip out and start blubbering all over me, let's just sit back and take a deep breath. You see, my friends, my illness is dreaded fear. To be precise, it's fear of old age. Go ahead and laugh, but believe me when I say, it is no laughing matter to me.

I have been sailing through life very confident that I had not yet been hit by old age. So what in the hell happened? Well, here's the rest of the story. In early 2014, I had cataract surgery on both eyes and it was very successful, so they tell me. Now, all of a sudden, I can see fine lines, crinkles, wrinkles and puffy eyes with raccoon circles. I tell myself this all just popped up overnight, but the whole truth is that they have been there all along. I just couldn't see that well.

All this time, 83 years to be accurate, I thought I was looking great, when all along I looked exactly like someone who is 83 years old. Talk about ego. Who in the hell did I think I was that I would escape the ravages of old age? I guess I really thought I was someone special!

I vividly remember my mother asking me to take her to the drug store to look at a new wrinkle reducer or some new skin lotion and I would actually get a little annoyed. Every new item that came on the market was in her vanity drawers. Her "beauty" items took up all the drawers in the double vanity in the main bathroom. Many times I asked her, "Mother, is this really necessary?" She would look at me over her glasses and roll her eyes. "Yes, I have no intention of looking like an old shriveled up prune."

I'm going to be very honest here. I'm at least three times worse than she ever was. The amount of money I spend on lotions of all kinds and cosmetics would feed a family of four. Money is no object. I'm high maintenance. The cosmetics I buy are top of the line, Origins and Clinique, and I have been using them for at least forty years. Actually, I'm afraid to stop using these fine products for fear I will, one fine morning, wake up looking like a prune that has been left in the drying machine way too long. Now I find out I look like that anyway, in spite of the thousands of dollars that I've spent trying not to look like a dried up prune. Bear in mind, the thousands of dollars were spent just on my face. My hair and clothing were a completely different matter.

While I was working, I kept a book of outfits that I wore. My goal was to wear an outfit one day and not wear it again for at least three weeks. Yes, I really had that many outfits. And if you know me at all, you know this is the absolute truth.

My motto, and I should have it tattooed on my butt, is always look your very best. I shower before I go to the gym, hair, light make-up, the whole nine yards. After I get back home, I shower again. The truth is I never leave my bedroom in the morning unless I'm showered, made up and dressed. Who wants to sit and have coffee first thing in the morning with a wrinkled, disheveled old lady? Even my children, who I know love me, will start to notice and get upset because Mom is getting old.

Now my daughter is another story. I am thoroughly convinced that I was given the wrong baby when I left the hospital all those years ago. The more time I spend with her, the more convinced I am.

She gets up in the morning, washes her face, pulls her hair back and goes to exercise class six days a week. Oh yes, before she leaves, she has coffee with her Dad and they both look like they crawled out of a cave. After exercise class, she gets back home, eats breakfast, sits at the table and balances her checkbook. By this time, it is about 12:30. Then she decides to run to Macy's as is, no shower, no change of workout clothes. How can she do that? This can't possibly be my daughter. What happened to that old saying, "the apple doesn't fall far from the tree?"

I once got into trouble when my granddaughter was about six years old. One day we were hanging out in the bathroom getting her ready for school and I told her, quite solemnly, a lady never leaves her house without Ludbriderming it up. Arms, legs, feet, chest and whatever else you want nice and smooth. Many mornings she was late getting down for breakfast because she was busily applying Lubriderm to various parts of her body. She is now 31 and it is still part of her beauty regimen.

Like I told you, I do not leave my bedroom unless I am completely dressed. Donald Trump could be sitting in my living room patiently waiting to discuss election strategy with me and I would keep him waiting. If I wake up with chest pains, before I am taken to the hospital, I will have to take a shower and fix my hair and put on clean pajamas.

I think you can get the picture. This is who I am and when I tell you I am fearful of old age, believe it. The other morning I looked at myself in the bathroom mirror and my mother was looking back at me with a little snicker on her face. "Don't forget to pull that white hair from the side of your face, Miss Smarty Pants," she says. A white hair growing out of my face? This is huge! Do reasonable women commit suicide over a hair growing on their face? Who in the hell ever said I was reasonable when it came to my appearance? You have to feel like you're the best looking, well put together broad in the entire room.

However, things they are a changing. Now that I can see better, I'm more aware than ever. I am God awful certain that one day I will wake up, look in the mirror and decide I am never going to leave my house again.

That day is fast approaching. Believe it when I readily admit, I am an extremely vain control freak bitch, but I wouldn't have it any other way!

MEN - OH - PAWS

Throughout the ages, women have always been referred to as the weaker sex. Why?? Is it because we can't bench press 300 or 400 pounds of weight? I'm still doing research on that. Anyway, why would anyone in their right mind want to do that?

Ages ago,   the term weaker sex might have been appropriate because no one knew any better. But now, I'm not so sure.

Past history tells us that women had very little to say. Before young girls even grew up, they married, had babies, cooked and cleaned and did heavy farm chores. If they had an opinion about something, a scathing look from the man of the house would immediately silence them.

Yes, the weaker sex. Ever see a picture of a big muscular farmer plowing up his field using his tiny wife as his plow horse? She was even properly clothed in a long dress covered up by an equally long white apron.

Time marched on and low and behold, women were permitted to vote. Wow, the powers to be (the men) finally realized women had brains and were capable of making decisions. Yeah for our side!

During World War II, women held meaningful jobs in defense factories so the men could go off to war. I'm sure we all remember the poster of that famous gal, Rosie the Riveter! We've come a long way baby!

Eventually women were in all facets of the workforce - professors, bankers, lawyers, accountants, and even doctors. Some women went so far as to own their own businesses. A lot of women even smoked cigarettes and could throw down a shot of whiskey as good as any man.

Finally, we were equal. Maybe not salary wise, but we could do the same jobs as our counterparts. Still couldn't bench press 300 or 400 pounds, but no one cared.

The bodies of women are different than men and I don't mean physical appearance. Our teenage years brings on the monthly scourge and that's so much fun! As a young girl I would hear my mother and aunts talking about how "they fell off the roof" and I didn't get it. How could they possibly fall off the roof so often and not get hurt? I was 13 years old when I finally figured it out. No, I wasn't dying, it was just part of becoming a woman.

Is there any woman out there who can truthfully say she enjoyed this monthly annoyance? Did you enjoy the cramps and the bloating? Why don't men get to enjoy this?

Women marry, get pregnant and have babies. Another wonderful experience. Anyone who has gone through childbirth knows we are definitely not the weaker sex. Is there a man alive who would live through hours and hours of hard labor? I think not. I'm sure the husbands were all exhausted after pacing the floor waiting for the little woman to bring a new life into the world.

So we raise our children and we are in our middle fifties. The best years of our lives. What comes knocking at our doors ... menopause or "the change" rears its ugly head. The only good thing about it is you can enjoy unlimited sex without fear of getting pregnant. Oh, goody!!

With this "change" comes mood swings, weight gain and the dastardly hot flashes and night sweats. You can be happily working at your desk looking absolutely perfect and it takes a swing at you. Heat rises from your feet and travels up your entire body to your head. Your upper lip is all sweaty, you feel the beads of moisture rolling down your back and your armpits are moist. The hair at the nape of your neck and by your ears is all wet. Your eyes dart around to see if anyone notices. No one has ever made a comment, but I bet they wondered about it, especially if they were male. Mind you, this is more than a once per day occurrence. My favorite aunt kept a man's handkerchief shoved down the front of her bra and she would pull out the hanky, say a few swear words and mop her face and chest As a kid, I thought it was pretty funny. Little did I know.

Daytime hot flashes are bad enough, but you haven't lived until you have night sweats. They wake you up from a fitful sleep. Your night clothes are damp with perspiration and, if you get out of bed and run your hand on the sheet, you can feel the outline of your body. This, too, is not a onetime event. It happens at least three or four times each and every night. Doesn't matter how warm or cold it is outside or in your room, it happens.

For lucky me, this has been going on for approximately 43 years, no relief at all. Shouldn't the hot flashes and night sweats stop at some time? Mine aren't. Every night I dress up in my fancy pajamas and crawl in bed. I could be cold, but in 15 or 20 minutes, here it comes and I have to throw off the covers. The temperature in the house is 64 degrees, my husband is buried under a mound of blankets and I'm completely uncovered.

Half way through the night, I get hit again and I feel like I can't breathe. I'm very hot so I whip off my pajama bottoms and throw them violently across the room. I have made one request of my husband. If he ever has to call 911 for me in the middle of the night, he has to put my pajama bottoms on first and then call. I don't want the EMTs to think badly of me. I swear this is going to be the cause of my death.

No man could tolerate this discomfort. Some men go nuts when they flush from Niacin doses and those flashes don't happen all that often.

I did a little research and men also go through a "change" called Andropause. There are no hot flashes or night sweats or mood swings. I think it just makes them drink more beer and their bellies get bigger. Besides that, they start losing their hair but, oddly enough, it starts growing out of their ears and nose. White, wiry hairs will emerge from their eyebrows and these strands keep growing and growing. If not cut, these strands start to curl. You could almost use these hairs for a comb-over.

So now they are in Andropause. They all secretly desire buying a really fast sports car and they like to ogle the young girls. They become fascinated by boobs. Now their hair can be cut with a pair of cuticle scissors, but what delays the process is the trimming of the ears, nose and eyebrows. And if they feel frisky, there's always that little blue pill. Wouldn't you like to be a fly on the wall in the emergency room after something lasts more than four hours?

Does this constitute the "change" for men? Must be really tough to go through all this.

Why is what women go through called MENOPAUSE?? What do men have to do with this condition? Most, if not all of them, don't understand it and can care less. What is it that the men are pausing?

Somebody, please come up with another name!!

MY MEMORIES OF CHRISTMAS

Christmas has always been a magical time of the year for me. As children, my brother and I would go to bed and there would be no tree in the living room. We were told if Santa thought we were good, he would come with the tree and presents. Boy, did we ever believe. As soon as our heads hit the pillow, we were sound asleep.

In the morning, my dad would come into our rooms and wake us up. Being the oldest, I had lots more to say than my brother. "Did he come? Did he bring presents? We were really good so I'm sure he came!" Dad would just smile and take our hands and lead us downstairs.

We would go down to the living room and there would be a very tall tree with many colored lights and icicles dangling from all the branches. A bright gold star was at the very top. Underneath the tree would be presents, all unwrapped because Santa is way too busy to wrap everyone's toys. What a wonderful day we would have. It was magic!

As I grew up, I knew there was no Santa Claus, only people who loved you unconditionally. I found different things to fill my heart. I love the bright holiday lights and the hustle and bustle in the mall. I love to walk the Main Street in Milford and listen to the Christmas music being played for everyone to enjoy. What is better than the smell of a freshly cut evergreen tree or nowadays, to be more practical, the scent of a burning evergreen candle? Decorating the tree with hundreds of ornaments is always fun, but I always think we need more ornaments. How do you feel when you see a toddler sitting on Santa's lap in the Mall? Do you see the expression on the child's face? What better experience is there than Midnight Mass with all the songs and pageantry!

Christmas is carols, both old and new. It means seeing family and dear friends. How about the wonderful smell of freshly baked cookies? Who can resist that! Who can resist the wonderful feel good Christmas stories on television? I'm sure we all wish we were in those stories

With our children all grown and with families of their own, we do the traveling. Everyone seems so happy. And this brings me to an extremely emotional experience I had in the Atlanta airport and it has happened two years in a row. This experience really makes me feel blessed.

After landing at Hartsfield Airport, we got on the train to go to the baggage area to get our bags and meet our children. As we got off the train, I could hear a distant rumble and the tile floor was vibrating. The sound came closer. The vibration grew stronger. The hallway was quite crowded with people getting off the train, but all of a sudden, up ahead, it was like Moses and the parting of the Red Sea.

The sound I heard was about six platoons of soldiers marching, all in step, backs straight, clean shaven and eyes forward. Everyone stopped in their tracks and made way for these fine young men and women. Everyone started to shout and clap as they passed by. I looked around and people were wiping their eyes, both men and women, young and old.

I came to find out later that the military units were passing through Atlanta on their way to be deployed to Afghanistan. There was a huge movement of troops and we were in the middle of it.

There would be no decorated trees in their houses or burning evergreen candles because they would be living in a tent. Their Christmas lights might be mortar fire streaking across the sky. These young men and women and, believe me they were young, were giving up their holiday so I could enjoy mine.

We should all bow our heads and give thanks that there are people out there who give up a part of their lives to keep us out of harm's way. God Bless Them All and keep them safe!

THE RANTINGS OF A MAD WOMAN

Hold on a minute! I have to get a ladder. My soap box is getting pretty tall and I don't want to fall. Well, that might be something for a new story, who knows!

Tell the truth, people! Are there things in your life that drive you crazy and you keep asking yourself why does it have to be like this? Annoying things, especially for the senior citizen group.

Sometimes I think about plotting some type of revenge, but chances of meeting any of these asinine creatures is slim and no way is that going to happen.

What am I ranting about? Well, I'm going to tell you. You didn't think for one moment you could stop me, did you?

I despise the marketing industry. You know, those snotty nosed young people who design packaging. You can tell they're artistic just by the way they wear their damn hair. They are like a bunch of clones. Of course, they are all very young and can't even imagine or don't care to imagine what old age means. You know, when the fingers don't operate properly and you can't even button up your own shirt. You almost have to carry an oil can at all times. Geez, if that would only work, my problems would be solved and I wouldn't have to plot the demise of the entire marketing industry.

What happened that put a bee in my underpants? Picture this scenario. My husband cut his finger and it was bleeding a lot. We are in the bathroom so I reach for the bandaids. I have them in all sizes, just in case. Guess what happens! I can't get the wrapper off the damn thing. There are arrows showing how to pull the edge of the wrapper, but it refuses to open. So I reach for another one.

I run into the kitchen for a pair of scissors to cut the wrapper. In the meantime, blood droplets are falling on the rug. Thank God the rug is red and it will blend in. Finally, I get the wrapper opened and fix up the cut.

It's only a damn bandaid. Opening it is not going to set off a nuclear explosion or start World War III. So why does it have to be so difficult? Somewhere there is a minion sitting behind his desk thinking of ways to aggravate the old folks.

Let's talk about packaging. Ever buy a new curling iron that is all encased in some type of hard plastic? You need a hacksaw to break through the plastic shell. So what if you lose a finger or slice your hand? That little minion is peeing his pants laughing.

Let's take packaging in another direction. What do you think of the plastic lotion and shampoo containers? You never, never get all the stuff out.

I'll give you a perfect example, as if you could stop me. I'm on a rant now. I purchased a 6-ounce plastic container of China-Gel, a topical pain reliever, similar to Ben Gay. After about two weeks, no matter what I did, I couldn't get another squirt out of the container. In desperation I took an Exacto knife and cut the plastic container in half. Talk about shock! Was I hallucinating as senior citizens tend to do from time to time?

There was gel in the lower half of the container. I took a spoon and scraped and scraped it all out, every last bit. How much did I get? I managed to spoon out 1/3 of a cup of China-Gel into a small plastic glass. I just went into the kitchen to check my measuring cup and 1/3 of a cup is about 2 1/4 or 2 1/2 ounces. I have been using the scrapings for about two weeks and I still have a little left and to think that, before I got desperate and cut the container, it would have gone into the garbage. I paid $21 for a 6-ounce container and would have been able to use only 3 3/4 ounces.

I don't know how that problem can be corrected. Maybe there should be a reminder on the container. If you know something is still hiding in the container, please be sure to cut it in half and get the remainder of what you paid for.

My ranting and raving must come to a stop now. I'm doing laundry and I have to go cut the top half off the soap container so I can finish the job.

Meanwhile back in their corner offices, the marketing demons are plotting to keep us from eating, taking our meds and God only knows what else. Instead of feeding us green crackers, they are just going to make it impossible to open anything. We will starve to death and we will be found all shriveled up and people will wonder what ever happened to these poor souls.

SAD THOUGHTS

Here it is, nine months later, and I'm back in the Surgical Lounge waiting for my husband's surgery to be over. This is the one thing I really despise. The waiting!

The other thing I hate is having to be brave. What I would like to do is hide in a dark closet, cry and hit something. This is very difficult, but I have to put on a happy face or he will be afraid and I don't ever want him to be fearful.

I start talking, non-stop, about anything and everything. It's very early, but I'm sure I can keep him occupied so he is worry-free for the most part. Our son has flown in from Kansas City so I will not be alone. He knows me so well; I catch a wink because he knows what I am doing with the non-stop talking and from time to time, he will join in.

We get to the hospital with ten minute to spare, proceed to the check-in desk and are cheerily greeted by the Admitting Clerk. There are the dreaded papers to fill out and Gene looks confused. He seems to not know the answers to some of the health questions, so I take the papers and we fill out the forms together. Finally, that's done and a male nurse comes to get him ready for the procedure.

As he walks out of the doorway, he looks back and gives me this fearful look as if he won't ever see me again and my heart aches. After an hour, the nurse comes to get me and tells me I can stay with him until he's given a nerve block, but then I can return to sit with him until it's time for surgery.

I find him joking with the nurses, so I feel better. Soon it is time for the nerve block and I am sent back to the waiting room. In 20 minutes, the nurse comes back to get me and our son and we find him partially asleep, but he raises his head and asks our son about his sleep machine.

"I need my machine to sleep you know. Please put it under my bed."

The sleep machine has been left in the car until it is needed, but we assure him that we will put it under his bed. That problem has been solved.

In comes a parade of people, two surgical nurses, the anesthesiologist and finally the very handsome doctor comes in and goes over the entire procedure with us.

Next comes the operating room nurse, Mike, and we go over medical history again. Blood sugar is great, but there is concern about the kidneys. They will be switching part of his pain medication for another that is not harmful to the kidneys, which is the main concern.

Very thorough and totally on top of everything. I make certain no dye will be used for contrast because of the kidneys and we are all in agreement.

So here we sit in this huge, cold waiting room and the chart on the wall shows that Patient #390 is now in surgery. Seems to be a slow day at Huron Valley Hospital. There are only four of us in here waiting, but I am sure more people will be coming in very soon.

If we are lucky and everything goes according to plan, Gene may be coming home later today. That will be great because I know he doesn't like to be anywhere I'm not. This makes me reflect on our past life together.

After almost 62 years of marriage, you'd think we'd be tired of one another, but that honestly is not the case. Looking back, marriage is not hard work or, at least, not as hard as some make it out to be.

Communication and compromise are two words that come to mind. There are other words such as kindness, compassion, responsibility, honesty and respect. If you are fortunate to have children and there is a problem, agree with one another and, if one of you disagrees, talk it out in private, never in front of the children. Kids learn at a very young age how to play one parent against the other for their own benefit. I have seen this put a real strain on several friends' marriages.

Sixty-two years with this man and every day is a gift from God. We have fun, we go everywhere together. We can go to McDonalds for coffee (part of our morning routine) and just sit in a booth talking for an hour. We are comfortable.

No one truly knows what the future holds for us. One of us will die before the other and it will be devastating. There will be such a sense of loss because our true soul mate will be gone from this earth. Suddenly your life will be turned upside down.

The list of "no mores" will be endless. No more coffee time or cozy restaurant dinners, no more talks about events that you wouldn't tell another living person, no more afternoon tea and cookies, no more after dinner ice cream cones, no more sitting together in a room, not saying a word, but being absolutely happy and at peace, no more football games where I'm screaming at the television and he's laughing at me, no more trips to Kensington Park where we frequently have picnics, just the two of us.

However, there is one big regret. If only we had met sooner, then we could have loved each other longer.

SPRING

I have patiently been waiting for spring since Christmas. I have been looking forward to warm and sunny days when the sky is a deep blue and the clouds are like puffs of cotton lazily moving in the sky.

Spring means you can start cleaning up the yard and all the flower beds and always and most importantly to me, wash windows.

Clean windows are at the top of my list. My mother taught me, when I was about 9 years old, to iron my Daddy's handkerchiefs and wash the windows. I really like to clean the windows, ironing is another matter.

As I grew up, I would keep the windows in the house shining and I suppose I did a darn good job because my favorite aunt always invited me over to do hers at least twice a year. She always insisted I use straight white vinegar with newspaper to wipe the windows dry and I really wasn't in favor of that. My hands would get all black from the newsprint and the acrid smell of the vinegar made my eyes water, but I did as I was told.

My family home was a two story one and I felt so grown up when I cleaned the bedroom windows. Open the window, put the rags and vinegar out on the roof, climb out the window onto the roof, have someone close the window and clean away. This was great.

The side upstairs windows were another matter. I would have to sit on the window sill to clean the outside and had to rely on my younger brother to hang on to my legs. I made sure never to do windows if we were mad at each other

At that time, I really thought it would be great to be a wife. Gee, I could wash windows whenever I wanted. Was I insane? It never occurred to me that there was a lot more to being a wife than washing windows.

I do not like to go into a restaurant that has dirty windows. Sometimes it just can't be helped. We are only weeks into spring and I have washed my windows twice already. Can anyone else say that?

The second best thing about spring is buying and planting flowers. Take me to a greenhouse and I go berserk. If I ever win the Lottery, I shall hire a semi-trailer, go to the greenhouse and say, load it up. I want it all.

Somehow it hasn't sunk into my brain that if you buy it, you have to plant it. You just don't wiggle your nose, a magical fairly appears and suddenly all the flowers you had to have are planted. When I was much younger, I planted at least 20 flats of annuals and at least 10 new perennials a year. Last weekend I planted 2 flats of flowers, it took me two hours, and I couldn't move all week. I now have to crawl along the flower beds on hands and knees because I can't bend over that much.

Another one of my favorite spring time activities is trimming tree branches. I even have my very own cross cut saw and it is one of my prize possessions. I painted the handle pink so everyone would know not to touch it or use it. It's mine!

When I first retired, my husband would come home from work and find our 2 1/2 acres of land littered with tree branches. You know, trim, drop them on the ground and walk away. I don't do clean-up.

Twenty years have passed since I retired and time is creeping up. It is really difficult to plant all those flowers. It is nearly impossible to carry the ladder to a tree, climb up and trim away. I do believe the rungs on the ladder have gotten further apart.

You will all laugh, but I know I have a character flaw. I want everything done at once. I found out it just ain't gonna happen anymore. Years ago I could go outdoors at 8 a.m., stop for lunch and by 5 o'clock I was done with the flower planting. I would sit back and admire my handiwork.

Just this past week-end, I started planting at 10:30 a.m. Well, after all, we had to go out for breakfast. By lunch time, only 2 flats of flowers had been planted and that was it for the day. Instead of 20 flats of flowers, I bought 8 and 3 new perennials. I feel sad about that, but there is nothing I can do about it. Yes, I have a backup plan this year as I did last year. A friend would be only too happy to help me out, but I'm not giving up.

I fully realize that at the rate I'm going, I should plant my last flower around August 1st.

But my windows sure are clean!

WHO SAYS??

There is a world famous rock and roll star who most assuredly will be in the Rock & Roll Hall of Fame someday in the future and his name is Jon Bon Jovi. He recorded a hit song entitled "Who Says You Can't Go Home!" I am here to testify that you can do exactly that! Don't let anyone tell you otherwise!

One fine day at a family gathering, I casually mentioned getting a notice regarding my 64th high school class reunion back in Windber, Pennsylvania. My oldest son piped up and said to make plans, I should definitely go and he would fly in from Seattle, Washington and drive me and his Dad. I was excited - at first - and then changed my mind at least a dozen times. Michael made his plane reservations and kept reminding me to make hotel reservations and get the paperwork into the reunion committee to let them know I would be there.

Without giving me a chance to agree or disagree, he casually told my brother what we were doing and he and his wife jumped on the bandwagon. He also told my mother's family (first and second cousins) and my brother got on Facebook and informed my father's family (first, second and third cousins). Most of them lived in the immediate area but some came from Mechanicsburg, Pennsylvania and Berea, Ohio, and everyone was very excited that we were coming for a visit. A giant snowball was rolling down the hill and I couldn't stop it.

Oh how I wanted to back out! Why did I ever open my mouth about the reunion? Back home was not a particularly happy place after my father died. Too damn many control freaks in my life telling me what to do. You know how it goes - "What will the neighbors think?" "You can't go out with him, he's not Catholic and he had on brown shoes with a navy blue suit." Not pleasant!

My son informed me that we should stay at the Hampton Hotel in Johnstown, Pennsylvania and gave me a list of all the activities he had planned. After looking long and hard at the list, I wrote a note to the reunion chairperson and told her that, even though I would be in town that weekend, I would be unable to attend the class reunion. The deed was now done - no backing out now except for death.

During the weeks leading up to D Day, I was not full of excitement or anticipation. My anxiety level was at an all-time high! Absolute dread would be a better word.

WEDNESDAY

We head to the airport early afternoon to pick up our designated driver and I'm asked a dozen times, "When are you going to pack?" I thought about this long and hard and know that I will be packing very casual clothing. These people are my family and I want everyone to be comfortable. No putting on the dog. So I pack, we have a nice dinner and by 10 p.m., we are all snuggled in because we are leaving early next day.

Thursday

I manage to stall and we don't leave until around 9:30 a.m. It's a six hour drive and it is quite enjoyable. We talk non-stop. Once more I'm told what our schedule will be and, by this time, my head is ready to explode. I must have had a moment of sheer insanity to ever agree to this trip. My son is driving and telling me "we're going to have a ball, Mom. You'll see. Just relax."

After about 5-1/2 hours, we are fast approaching our first stop, Central City, Pennsylvania, home of my cousin and God child, Bobby. Did I mention that he is a year older than Michael and is the only Funeral Director in this teeny 320 acre town of about 1200 people and, you guessed it, not a damn traffic light in the entire town? He is also one of two coroners for Somerset County. He and Michael are really tight and Michael has spent a lot of time there during the last three or four years. He loves the quietness of the town and the friendliness of all the people. I think he could run for Mayor and win by a landslide.

As we approach the funeral home parking lot, the street is full of people. In the middle of one group, I spy a familiar figure -- tall, thin, very bald and bearded. Yes, he's older and I haven't seen him since he buried my mother in 1993, but it's him. I'd know that mischievous grin anywhere.

He runs over and picks me up. "My God, Cuz, I thought you'd died and no one called to let me know. I was pissed until I found out you were still alive. Go on in, you know the way. Donna's upstairs and I'll be right there. Bet the undertakers don't look like this in Michigan."

Well, no. He had on flip flops, shorts, a white t-shirt and a baseball cap backwards. He let loose with a few choice profanities. Seems he has four funerals going on, three on display and one holding, so there will be two funerals Friday and a trip to the crematorium early Saturday morning. He and Michael will be busy.

My mind flashed back to my teenage years when I spent lots of time at the funeral home babysitting this grown up man standing in front of me. It was a semi-serious place back then, but now it is a light hearted atmosphere, at least upstairs in the living quarters. Lots of laughter, but I believe, in this line of work, it has to be that way!

I run upstairs to greet the lady of the manor and take a quick tour of the area. An apartment of two bedrooms and a bathroom have been added and Michael informs me that is his living quarters. The furniture is all different, of course, but the human skull and the lava rock are still on the shelf in the hallway. I remember referring to the skull as Rocky and it was on a desk in the room I always slept in when I stayed overnight. I would occasionally confide in Rocky and tell him my gripes. He never ever gave me any advice, although I once thought he winked at me.

So after spending some time here, we are off to check into our hotel and pick up the rental car for Michael and wait for my brother and his wife. Michael leaves to go back to Central City and gives us our marching orders for the next day.

My brother and wife finally arrive and we are very excited to see each other. He fills me in on all his many ailments. I do believe he's a hypochondriac and I cluck over him like a mother hen and he seems happy for the attention and then we're off to dinner.

FRIDAY

Friday morning dawns sunny and crisp. Since one of the perks of staying at a Hampton Hotel is breakfast, we venture down to the Lobby and we are immediately greeted by the heavenly smell of sugar and cinnamon. The huge breakfast bar is covered with plates of French toast sticks, scrambled eggs, western omelet squares, bake it yourself in two minutes waffles, toast, bagels, English muffins, blueberry muffins, fruit salad, bananas, apples, juice, milk, coffee and tea. I'm sure I've forgotten something. It was a breakfast buffet fit for a king and queen. We spend at least a half hour stuffing ourselves and then go back to our room to wait for a phone call from the brother.

Finally, he calls and tells me to meet them at Denny's. We join them for coffee and wait for St. Michael, the Archangel, to meet us. He has taken over the leadership role and has been taking it very seriously. He leaves his car and takes ours, but Brother Tom drives himself.

First stop, St. Anthony's Cemetery to visit my parents, grandparents and various other family members. The cemetery is up on a hill and you get a panoramic view of the town of 4,000 people. The leaves are starting to turn and it is truly beautiful. We have brought flowers for our parents' grave and we walk around trying to find various family members. The cemetery seems much smaller than it did when I was growing up, but I still, for the most part, can find my grandparents.

Next stop - Cousins Rosemary and Patty. But first - we must stop at Mama Leone's for at least three of her famous Italian submarine sandwiches to take for lunch at the cousin's house.

You have never eaten a submarine sandwich the likes of Mama Leone's. They are made on an entire loaf of fresh Italian bread which measures about 22 inches long. We order the subs and I'm talking to Mama Leone (who is 95 years old) while keeping a watchful eye on the sub maker. It's an art and I can't wait to sink my teeth into my part.

There are many different tastes that will mingle in my mouth - hard and genoa salami, capicola, prosciutto, provolone cheese, thinly sliced onions, lettuce, hot pepper rings and I'm sure I'm forgetting something. All of this is topped off with a perfect mixture of oil, vinegar and oregano drizzle. I can't wait for that first bite.

We drive the short distance to Patty's house and you'd think we were royalty. Patty had just had knee replacement surgery so she couldn't have been feeling that great. Sister Rosemary and her husband were there and, believe me when I say, we were welcomed with open arms. It was great catching up and eating Mama Leone's subs plus all the other food that magically appeared on the kitchen counter.

After about three hours, it was time to go onto the next adventure. We are off to the thriving metropolis of Central City to pick up Bobby and his wife, Donna. Pennsylvania is a gorgeous state. Lots of beautiful trees but narrow two lane highways - one lane going one way and the other lane going the other way. Some roads are even narrower and if you happen to meet a car going in the opposite direction, you close your eyes and say a quick prayer. I do believe the locals can spot a greenhorn on the road because they always manage to move over just enough for you to pass.

Here we are at the funeral home and we pile into Bobby's big SUV. There are seven of us, but we manage quite nicely. Donna takes the wheel and we're off to Shanksville, Pennsylvania, the September 11, 2001 crash site of Flight 93. This site is approximately 8 miles from Central City and about 12 miles from my hometown. We drive on some very narrow winding roads with huge farms dotting the landscape. Never saw so many red barns in a very long time. This is farm country and it is very picturesque.

We finally come up to the entrance and all that is there is a black and white sign that says "Flight 93." I guess that's all that needs to be said. The actual site is about three miles off the entrance and the area is huge with large clumps of trees almost surrounding a huge open grassy field. There is a newly opened museum up on a hill overlooking the crash site and huge brick walls have been constructed near the museum. These walls stand separate from one another with just enough space in between so that you can see the open field.

The museum is manned by military personnel and Pennsylvania State Troopers and, although there is no entrance fee, only six or seven people can enter at one time. In this way, the inside is not packed with people at any given time and you can really see what's on display.

The display starts out with the towers in New York City being hit and that is mostly newspaper articles. Then you get to the Flight 93 display. People stood and read every word on each display and no one spoke. There was an eerie hush in the room and when someone said something, it was done in a very quiet whisper.

The display cases had the voice recorder, bent and mangled silverware, a twisted tray, cell phones and too many other things to mention. They found a credit card belonging to one of the terrorists and that was how they were able to trace the money that funded this disaster. Ironically, the card was as it should be, not twisted like so much of the other things.

Finally we went outside and sat down off to the side. It was time for Bobby to start talking. Remember he was one of the two coroners immediately called to the scene on that dark day. He told us that the airplane landed upside down and all the luggage was all over the open field. He said the field was actually covered with yellow tags marking every piece of anything that was found. Nothing was unimportant.

DNA samples were gotten from the families and every piece of flesh, no matter how small, was tested. He told me one mother approached him and tearfully told him she hoped he would find her son. He had a tattoo of a submarine on his right arm. The arm was found and then he had to convey the horrible news to the mother. I don't know what I really thought, but I didn't think "our kids", as Bobby put it, were buried at this location.

Well, all the body parts from our 40 Americans are buried in a huge hole, right next to the crash site. There is a large boulder next to the burial site that marks the actual spot of the impact. There is a swatch of bare ground that marks the flight path of the incoming plane. I asked him what happened to the body parts of the terrorists. He told me we are Americans and we take care of our own. He immediately changed the subject.

We walked quite a distance to get to the burial site. There is a white brick curved wall with the name of each of the 40 Americans. A sidewalk runs behind the wall and there is a very tall wooden locked gate at the end. The path beyond the gate leads to the burial site and only family members can get in there.

This project is not complete yet. They have planted 40 beautifully shaped trees along the walkway and a Future Tower of Voices with 40 wind chimes is to be erected. Everywhere you look, you see a board erected with the 40 names. No one will ever forget! This was a common field one day and it will be a field of honor forever.

We finally end our tour and head back to Bobby and Donna's for dinner. Along the way, Donna tells us that the story in this small hamlet is that several farmers were out working in their fields and they swear they saw two F-16's peel off right as they saw and heard the explosion. Is that true? No one really knows and our government is not talking. Just think about this - the plane went down in an open field, two miles away from a school. Also, at the rate of speed the plane was traveling, 563 miles per hour, it would have reached Washington, D.C. - the Capitol or White House - who knows - in 18 minutes.

Food for thought - a friend told me that all air travel was banned that fateful day except for two F-16's out of Selfridge Field.

We are quiet on the ride back to Central City. What we saw will stick in our minds the rest of our lives.

Pulling into the parking lot at the funeral home, everyone started talking at once, but no one mentioned what we had just seen. Donna had planned a Polish dinner for us and while she finished up with dinner, Michael, Bobby and I went down to vacuum up the vacant rooms downstairs. My brother, Tom, stayed upstairs and helped with dinner. He still has a hard time being in the house, especially in the downstairs area. I do believe after I got married, he and my mother spent a lot of time at the funeral home and, being only 7 years old, it left a lasting mark on him.

Anyway, dinner was going to be delicious. The smell of stuffed cabbage and cabbage and noodles wafted downstairs and we hurried up with our vacuuming and went up to eat dinner. Oh yes, we had Donna's famous sweet smelling carrot cake with real cream cheese icing for dessert. I thought I had died and gone to heaven.

We have had a long day and it is now approaching 11 p.m. Time to hit the road. Bobby and Michael drive us to our hotel so Michael can pick up his rental car and he tells us to go straight to bed. Tomorrow will be another big day, bigger than today. Can't wait.

SATURDAY

Another picture perfect day! We bypass the heavenly smells of the Hampton breakfast bar because we're meeting Brother Tom and his wife for breakfast at Denny's.

After breakfast, we are due to meet Michael at my old high school, Windber High School, Home of the Windber Ramblers - Siss, Boom, Bah!! Over the years, a large addition was put on the original part and now the old part where I walked the hallowed halls, is to be torn down and a new state of the art building is to be erected. Can't figure that out - population 4,000 - how many kids of high school age can there be? I heard a rumor that Windber will merge with Shade Township so that explains it all.

We find Michael waiting in front of the school and we start the tour. It has been 64 long years since I last entered the front door. The tour is sad. All I can see is ugly Rambler Blue lockers lining the hallways. We didn't have lockers, we had coat rooms and we carried our books from class to class or left them in home room. I can't remember the halls being so narrow or the stairways so steep and confining. I remember having a class on the first floor and running like a fool to get to the opposite end of the third floor before the bell rang. It was all we knew so we did what was necessary.

After about 40 minutes of touring, we're done and it is almost noon, time to travel to the Windber Grand Hotel - a full half mile away - and meet all the Marfizo relatives. Sixteen of us will be having lunch together and some I haven't seen in more than 20 years.

The biggest surprise was Bob and Carol. Bob is not a relative of mine per se, but he is the uncle of all my cousins on their mother's side. We went to school together for 12 years. When we were in the 8th grade, he took me to a school dance and we had fun. He was a shirt tail relative so, although he was part of our extended family, we didn't date again. It would have been like dating your cousin or brother. We were good friends all through school and then we both moved on. He reminded me that he had always looked out for me and we should have dated more when we were in high school. I reminded him, in front of his second wife, that he was busy dating my friend, Betty Lou, and they got married shortly after graduating. Unfortunately, Betty Lou died at a very young age and he was left along with two very small children. By that time, I had married my Marine and got the hell out of Dodge.

The next wonderful surprise was my cousin, Bill. He is one year younger than I and we were close. The only problem was that he was always in some kind of trouble and if one of our teachers asked if he was my brother, I would cringe and violently shake my head. He told me he always felt sorry for me when the principal would send me to get him and bring him back to the office. We had a very good laugh over that.

He played football, went to William & Mary College in Williamsburg, Virginia and became a very successful oral surgeon. He lives in Mechanicsburg and, as I looked at him, I thought, *damn, sure wish I knew the name of his plastic surgeon. He looks fantastic.* His second wife is much younger and a very pretty blonde with long hanging hair so he has to keep up. Believe it or not, her name is Angel.

What a great family I have. It's like the years away from each other fell away and we had just seen each other the week before. We had a four hour lunch and no one was bored.

We say our good byes until we meet again next year and Gene, Brother Tom and Terri and I go back to our hotels to rest. Tonight we will be having dinner at a great Italian restaurant with my mother's side of the family. So we all go to our respective corners for some much needed rest.

Before you know it, the time has come to leave for dinner. We are going to Rizzo's Famous Italian Restaurant, the town hot spot almost every night, and especially Saturday nights.

Growing up, I hung around with Johnny and Mary Lou who lived in the apartment above the restaurant. It was called Rillo's then and it was just as popular then as it is now. I spent quite a lot of time there during my high school years and had quite a few dishes of pasta there. This is going to be fun, like going back in time.

We pull into the parking lot and I see part of my family waiting in line by the back door. People are lined up on the sidewalk and there are people sitting on the stairs going up to the restaurant. The hostess spies Bobby and we are taken into a large semi-private room where we are joined by Brother Thomas, his wife, and our cousin, Janet. About five minutes go by and I hear a squeal and it is my cousin, Missy, and her husband, Billie. She is Bobby's sister and the two of them together should be on Saturday Night Live. Conversation is flowing from all areas of the table, everyone is talking at the same time. Funny thing, we all seem to be following all of the conversation.

Three waitresses are going to handle our wild bunch and we order. Wine is ordered, 3 liters of fine Italian wine, three separate glasses of white wine, three large heaping antipasto platters, about four orders of Wedding Soup and all my favorite dishes....eggplant and veal parmigiana, ravioli, spaghetti and meatballs and my mouth is watering just thinking about the heavenly food.

The antipasto is fresh and crisp with lettuce, salami, fresh mozzarella cheese, olives and hot peppers. The fresh basil smell is wonderful and we all dig in. Next comes the main courses and they are a sight to behold. Not only does all the food look scrumptious, the smell is out of this world, fresh tomato sauce, a hint of garlic and basil and the pungent odor of Pecorino Romano grated cheese. I am so excited to get the first bite and it does not disappoint. Being family, we start passing our plates around so everyone can have a taste. Haven't done that in such a long time and, you know what, it's kind of nice. Between mouthfuls, we still keep talking. Damn wonder one of us didn't choke from eating, talking and laughing. Let's not forget the many glasses of wine!

Finally, we're done eating! Hang on to your seats, that scrumptious meal for ten people cost a whopping $229. Only in Windber, Pennsylvania could that happen.

The evening is over and we all head back to wherever we'll be sleeping. We don't have big plans for Sunday. Sleep late, eat breakfast, take Michael's car back to the rental agency and head for Central City. Donna is cooking us an Italian meal and our tour guide says we'll be leaving to head back to Milford at 1 o'clock.

We get to Central City around 11 a.m. and do some more kitchen table visiting. Friends come in to see Bobby and they join in the conversation. This is what I love most about this place. Dinner is at 11:30 a.m. and it is awesome, stuffed shells and sauce and mouthwatering meatballs, a beautiful tomato and cucumber salad and more carrot cake for dessert. I wish I had taken a picture of the salad. The tomatoes were home grown and big and juicy. This gal can cook.

Finally it is 1 o'clock and Michael signals that it is time to head for Michigan. We sadly say our goodbyes and promise to return soon and we're on our way. The ride to the Pennsylvania Turnpike is through a very rural area, few houses and very narrow windy roads but we make it. We're on our way!

It's a great ride, first on the Pennsylvania Turnpike and then the Ohio Turnpike. The Pennsylvania Turnpike is windy, lined with beautiful changing trees and the Ohio Turnpike is quite flat with not so many trees. A driver could easily doze off in Ohio, no hairpin curves, no high bridges to cross.

Non-stop talking is going on the entire trip. We make two stops and I enjoy a caramel Frappuccino with whipped cream at both rest areas. Thank goodness for Starbucks.

It's 8 p.m. and we pull into our driveway. It was a wonderful trip. For all my complaining, I'm so happy we went back home. You can go home. It's like you never left. Now I'm homesick big time. I miss the way of life my family leads. I miss the camaraderie with the neighbors and almost everyone you meet. Like the saying goes, you never meet a stranger! Would I move back? You will be surprised, but I absolutely would in a heartbeat.